ISLAMIC LEGAL MAXIMS

Consisting of Al-Karkhi's Al-'*Usul*

Arabic text, English transliteration and English translation, notes and a short historical and biographical introduction

Justice Dr. Munir Ahmad Mughal

istinarah Press

Instinarah Press

MaktabaIslamia Publications

www.maktabaislamia.com
info@maktabaislamia.com
www.facebook.com/everythingislamic
www.twitter.com/maktabaislamia

2017 CE – 1438 H

Translation of the Qur'ān

It should be perfectly clear that the Qur'ān is only authentic in its original language, Arabic. Since perfect translation of the Qur'ān is impossible, we have used the translation of the meaning of the Qur'ān throughout the book, as the result is only a crude meaning of the Arabic text.

Qur'ānic verses appear in speech marks proceeded by a reference to the Surah and verse number. Sayings (*Hadith*) of Prophet Muhammad ﷺ appear in inverted commas along with reference to the Hadith Book and its Reporter.

صلى الله عليه وسلم #- ﷺ(Peace be upon him)

سبحانه وتعالى #- ﷻ(Glory to Him, the Exalted)

Contents

Preface

Before the establishment of Pakistan the slogan of all Muslims in India was:

Pakistan ka matlab kiya
La Ilaha Illallah –Muhammadur Rasulullah.

By the Grace of Allah (swt) Almighty, the struggle of the Muslims under the leadership of *Quaid-i-Azam* Muhammad 'Ali Jinnah, Pakistan was established as a national homeland for the Muslims on 14th of August 1947. The object of establishment of Pakistan was that the Muslims in Pakistan would be enabled individually and collectively to order their lives in accordance with the teachings and tenets of Islam, as set out in the Holy Qur'an and Sunnah. The objectives resolution of March 12, 1949 was passed for the same reason.

Allamah Iqbal had said:

"… And I have no doubt that a deeper study of the enormous legal literature of Islam is sure to rid the modern critic of the superficial opinion that the law of Islam is stationary and incapable of development…" [1]

By the Grace of Allah (swt) during last fifty years we are heading towards the Islamization of Law in Pakistan. Institutions like the Islamic Research Institute, Islamic Ideological Council, International Islamic University,

---

[1] Iqbal, Allamah Muhammad, The Reconstruction of Religious Thought in Islam, 2nd edn., Lahore: Institute of Islamic Culture, 1989, p. 131

Federal *Shari'at* Court, *Shari'at* Appellate Bench of the Supreme Court, the Legislature, the enforcement of Islamic Laws are all proof of this sincere effort. Both the state as well as the public desire the implementation of Islamic Injunctions. The present work is a humble attempt in this regard.

The oldest collection of Legal Maxims that has reached to us is the *Risalah* *'usul, al-Karkhi* (260AH-340AH)

By deep study of these *'usul* it reveals that they are inclusive of *qawa'id*, *dawabit*, *'usul*, and *kulliyat*. Some of them have the status of such general *kulliyat* that can be declared as the collective asset of Islamic *Fiqh* and some *'usul* are such which may be useful in knowing the effective cause of *Fiqhi* values and to know the solution of *Fiqhi* problems according to the Hanafi way of proving a thing (*istidlal*) and the Hanafi style of logical deduction on a legal question (*ijtihad*) by a learned and enlightened doctor (*Mujtahid*).

Imam al-Karkhi is the author of the first existing book on legal maxims.

Probably, in the said legal maxims, seventeen maxims of Imam of *Ahl al-Ra'i* Abu Tahir al-Dabbas, Al-Hafiz, al-Qadi, Muhammad bin Muhammad are also included who was a contemporary of Imam al-Karkhi. But it is difficult to point out exactly as to which were those seventeen principles of al-Dabbas in the collection of Al-Karkhi. [2]

"…The style of Imam Karkhi is that he states the legal maxim in a small

---

[2] Ghazi, Justice Dr. Mahmud Ahmad, *Qawa'id Kulliyyah aur un ka Aghaz wa Irtiqa'*, Islamabad: *Shari'ah* Academy, International Islamic University, 1992 (Publication no. 3), p. 36.

sentence while Imam Nasafi gives brief example. The principle and the example are so concise that a person who is not well-versed in *Fiqh* he is not in a position to easily get benefit of it. Here it should be remembered that the legal maxims of Imam Karkhi have undergone the process of refinement in the later centuries and almost all the maxims at present are not in their original shape that was given to them by Imam Karkhi. For instance, out of the ninety nine legal maxims given in Al-Majallah only one maxim (article no. 4 of Al-Majallah) is partially stated according to the form of the first maxim of *Al-'usul* of Imam Karkhi. Otherwise, all the remaining maxims are present in Al-Majallah so far as their meanings are concerned, but the words and statements are not the same which were given to them by Imam Karkhi."[3]

Each legal maxim begins with the word *"al-aslu"* (pl. *al-usul*), which literally means the root, the basis, the fundamental principle. Technically, it would mean the "basic rule is" or "the presumption is" or "it is to be presumed".

The Messenger of Allah (swt) (peace and blessings of Allah (swt) be upon him) has said that wisdom is the lost property of every believer and wherever it is found he deserves the most to have it. To make use of the available treasures of Legal Maxims should be welcome provided always that it is not repugnant to the injunctions of the Holy Qur'an and the Sunnah. The criteria for all times to come and for all purposes shall remain:

La ilaha illAllah (swt) Muhammad ur-Rasulullah.
"There is no God save Allah (swt) and Muhammad (saw) is the

---

[3] *ibid*, p.39.

Messenger of Allah"

O Allah (swt)! Send thy Blessings upon Muhammad and his family as thou sent blessings upon Ibrahim and his family. O Allah (swt)! Send thy benedictions on Muhammad and his family as thou sent benedictions on Ibrahim and his family.

With this view I have translated the `Arabic version of Al-`Usul of Imam Karkhi into English so that the legal fraternity throughout the world may get benefit from the light available from this source and a comparative study may be possible for the research scholars in the East and the West.

Alexander David Russell and `Abdullah al-Mamun Suhrawardy translated Bakurat al-Sa`d (First Steps in Muslim Jurisprudence) of Ibn Abu Zayd into English[4], which is a treatise on the Maliki law, and gave Arabic text along with the translation and gave two reasons. I also adopt the same reasons, which are reproduced with minor adaptations:

> a.   For the lawyer or administrator who is to take a useful part in the practical application of Muslim law, it is of the greatest importance, indeed one may almost say indispensable to have some acquaintance with the original…the fact must be recognized at the outset, that here is no shallow study to be taken up and mastered in a few weeks, but a vast science in which the genius of the same people which gave arithmetic, algebra, trigonometry, astronomy, optics, chemistry and medicine to the western world, and generally

---

[4] Russell, Alexander David and Suhrawardy, Abdullah al-Mamun, London: Luzac & Co., 1963, pp. viii - ix.

stood at the cradle of modern science, has exhibited in itself in all its power and exactitude. To acquire, therefore, the technology of the subject is the first and indispensable step towards sound knowledge; and for the encouragement of the beginner it may be added that, despite the marvelous and well-nigh inexhaustible richness of the Arabic language in the domain of belles lettres, the conventional language of Muslim law is by no means so copious or varied as to defy any really earnest student; while the justness and preciseness of its employment will even at an early stage rouse his appreciation.

b.   It may be useful both for the English readers and the Arabic scholars.

Justice Dr. Munir Ahmad Mughal

245 Circular Road, Lahore
Email: justice_mughal@hotmail.com

Shawwal 1419AH / January 1999 CE

Introduction

Definition of Legal Maxims (*Qawa 'id Al-Fiqhiyyah*)

Literal Definition

Al-Subki (d. 771AH) has given the literal definition of legal maxim as
under:

"al-qa'idatu al-asasu fa qawa'idu'l-bayti asasuhu."
"The word *al-qa'idatu* (pl. *al-qawa'id*) means foundation and *qawa'idu'l-bayt* means the foundations of a house."[5]

The wood fixed under the palanquin are also called *qawa'id* as those are
the foundations for it. The capital of a country is also called *al-Qa'idah* as
it is also significant like the foundation of a country.

The word al-qawa'idu has been used in the Holy Qur'an at three places,
viz.:

وَإِذْ يَرْفَعُ إِبْرَاهِيمُ الْقَوَاعِدَ مِنَ الْبَيْتِ وَإِسْمَاعِيلُ رَبَّنَا تَقَبَّلْ مِنَّا إِنَّكَ أَنتَ السَّمِيعُ الْعَلِيمُ

*"And remember Abraham And Isma'il raised The foundations of the House
(With this prayer): Our Lord! Accept (this service) from us: For Thou art the
All-Hearing, The All-Knowing."*   [TMQ Baqara:127]

---

[5] Al-Subki, Tajuddin 'Abd al-Wahhab, *Al-Ashbah wa'l-Naza'ir.*

قَدْ مَكَرَ الَّذِينَ مِن قَبْلِهِمْ فَأَتَى اللَّهُ بُنْيَانَهُم مِّنَ الْقَوَاعِدِ فَخَرَّ عَلَيْهِمُ السَّقْفُ مِن فَوْقِهِمْ وَأَتَاهُمُ الْعَذَابُ مِنْ حَيْثُ لَا يَشْعُرُونَ

"Those before them did also Plot (against Allah (swt)'s Way): But Allah (swt) took their structures from their foundations and the roof Fell down on them from above And the Wrath seized them From directions they did not perceive."
[TMQ AnNahl : 26]

وَالْقَوَاعِدُ مِنَ النِّسَاءِ اللَّاتِي لَا يَرْجُونَ نِكَاحًا فَلَيْسَ عَلَيْهِنَّ جُنَاحٌ أَن يَضَعْنَ ثِيَابَهُنَّ غَيْرَ مُتَبَرِّجَاتٍ بِزِينَةٍ ۖ وَأَن يَسْتَعْفِفْنَ خَيْرٌ لَّهُنَّ ۗ وَاللَّهُ سَمِيعٌ عَلِيمٌ

"Such elderly women as are Past the prospect of marriage,– There is no blame on them, If they lay a side Their outer garments, provided They make not a wanton display Of their beauty: but It is best for them To be modest: and Allah (swt) Is One Who sees and knows All things."
[TMQ An-Nur : 60]

Technical Definition

Technically, a legal maxim has a little different meaning than the maxims of other arts and sciences. For example, in grammar, physics and mathematics etc., a legal maxim refers to such value or principle that applies to all its particulars. In other words, it applies to all branches of such science. For example, the rules of grammar are,–

1. an active agent (*fa`il*) is always *marfu`*; and

2. a passive agent (*maf`ul*) is always *mansub*.

Both these rules cover all kinds of active agents and passive agents and are equally applicable to all of them. There is not a single active agent or passive agent that can be excluded from the application of these fundamental rules.

Likewise, the fundamental laws of physics, mathematics, logic, etc., apply in all circumstances to their sub-issues. For example, –

1.   Everybody continues in its state of rest or of uniform motion in a straight line except in so far as it is compelled by the impressed forces to change that state.

2.   The rate of change of momentum is proportional to the impressed force and takes place in the direction of the force.

3.   To every action there is an equal and opposite reaction.

4.   Two plus two make four.

5.   A whole is greater than any of its parts.

A legal maxim does not become applicable in all the circumstances and problems that may come under it. Rather it applies to most of its forms and many other forms remain excluded from its application. Therefore, in sciences other than *Fiqh*, a fundamental principle is defined in the following words:

"hukmun kulliyyun yantabiqu `ala jami`i juz'iyyatihi li ta`rafa ahkamuha minha."

"A fundamental principle is that general principle or law that applies to all particular forms to know the values regarding them by that principle."[6]

"Qadiyyatun kulliyyatun muntabiqatun 'ala jami' juz'iyyatihi"
"A general rule that is applicable to all its particulars (details / items)."[7]

As against it, the definitions of a legal maxim are such that due regard has been made in the definitions of the fact that its application is not on all the particular forms. Rather its application is on most of the particular forms.

Some definitions of legal maxims are reproduced below.

1. *"Hukmun akthariyyun la kulliyyun yantabiqu 'alaakthari juz'iyyatihi li ta'rafa ahkamaha minha."*

"A legal maxim is a fundamental principle that is not general in its application. Rather, it applies to the most of the particulars (details / items) that come under it so that the juristic value of such particulars (details) may be known by its application."[8]

2. *"Hukmun aghlabiyyun yantabiqu 'ala mu'zami uz'iyyatihi"*

"A legal maxim is a probable value and applies to the most of the particulars (items/details) coming under it."[9]

3. *"Hukmun kulliyyun au ghalibun yantabiqu 'ala juz'iyyati kulliha au aktharihu."*

---

[6] Al-Hamawi, *Sharh Al-Ashbah wa'l-Naza'ir*, Lakhnow: Nolkashor Press, p. 19.
[7] Muhammad Rawwas Qal'aji, *Mu'jam Lughatu'l-Fuqaha'*, Karachi, p. 354.
[8] ibid.
[9] *ibid.* Refer to by Allama Mustafa Ahmad al-Zarqa', *Al-Fiqh al-Islami fi Thaubihi al-Jadid*, Damascus, 1963, vol. II, p. 946.

"A legal maxim is a value which is general or probable which applies on all or majority of its particulars."[10]

4.   *"Huwa'l-hukmu'l-kulliyyu awi'l-akthariyyu allazi yuradu bihi ma`rifati hukmi'l-juz'iyyat."*

"A legal maxim is a value which is general or applicable to the most , the object of which is to know the particulars by it."[11]

5.   *"Hukmun kulliyyun yantabiqu `ala jami`i juz'iyyatihi li tu`arrafa ahkamuha minhu."*

"A legal maxim is such general value that applies to all its particulars so that their values are known."[12]

6.   *"Hukmun aghlabiyyun yuta`arrafu minhu hukmu'l-juz'iyyati al-Fiqhiyyati mubashiratan."*

"A legal maxim is a probable value whereby the values of juristic particulars are known directly."[13]

In all the above definitions, two things are common, viz.,

a.   The fundamental principles of *Fiqh* are called *kulliyyah* but in most of the cases they are not general. Rather they apply in most of the cases of particulars coming under them. This thing has been

---

[10] ibid.

[11] Ibn Rustam Baz, *Sharh al-Majallah,* chapter I.

[12] Ibn Khatib al-Dahshanah, *Mukhtasar Qawa`id al-`Ula'i.*

[13] Al-Muqri, Abu `Abdullah Muhammad bin Muhammad bin Ahmad, *Al-Qawa`id,* Makkah al-Mukarramah, p. 107.

given due regard in all the definitions.

b.   All the above definitions are useful knowledge for those who have concept of fundamental principles but those who have no concept of a fundamental principle, it is very difficult for them to have the correct concept of a legal maxim by the aid of these definitions.

For this reason, Dr. Mustafa Ahmad al-Zarqa' is not satisfied with the above definitions. In his opinion, none of the above definitions is such exhaustive, clear, and perfect that by the help of it a reader may get full awareness of the nature and reality of a fundamental principle. He has himself given a definition whereby the nature and reality of a fundamental principle becomes fully manifest. His definition is as under:

"Usulun Fiqhiyyatun kulliyyatun fi nususin mujizatin dasturiyatin tatadammanu ahkaman tashri'iyyatan 'ammatan fi'l-hawadith allati tadkhulu tahta maudu'iha."

"Legal maxims are those fundamental juristic principles that have been prepared in concise legal language whereby such general legal and juristic values are stated that are concerning the events (incidents) falling under that subject."

Kemal A. Faruki says:

"We have seen that, ultimately, *Qiyas* is the deduction from a *shari'ah* principle, of the *hukm* or *shari'ah* value, applicable to a new problem. Thus, the reasoning is from general principle to particular fact. But it is important to remember that the greater proportion, by far, of *Qiyas* rulings are not direct deductions from a *shari`ah* principle but are deductions from a case set out in *shari`ah* which exemplify a *shari`ah* principle, however unexpressed the full *shari`ah* principle may be. The movement of analogy, therefore, is usually from the original principle-exemplifying case to new case and only infrequently from principle itself, directly, to the new case. On those rare occasions when the analogy have been reached from the *shari`ah* principle direct to the new case, the *shari`ah* principle has been expressed in the form of a legal maxim. What may well be found necessary, to effectively apply *Qiyas* to the heavy problems facing it, is the encouragement of the development of maxims and of analogical deductions from principle to particular direct, instead of from a particular exemplifying the principle to the new particular."[14]

Allamah Hamawi has distinguished between a general principle and a fundamental principle. According to him, the definition of a fundamental principle is as under:

"Al-qawa`id allati lam tadkhul qa`idatum minha tahta qa`idatin ukhra, wa in kharaja minha ba`da'l-afrad."

"Fundamental principles are those principles out of which no fundamental principle falls under any other fundamental principle even if some of its own particulars remain excluded from it."[15]

---

[14] Faruki, Kemal A., *Islamic Jurisprudence,* Karachi: Pakistan Publishing House, 1962, p. 147.

[15] Al-Hamawi, *Ghamz `Uyun al-Basa'ir fi Sharh al-Ashbah wa'l-Naza'ir,* Luknow: Nolkashor Press, p. 19.

Difference between *usul ad-Din*, *usul al-Hadith*, *Usul al-Fiqh* (Principles of Jurisprudence) and *Qawa'id al-Fiqhiyyah* (Legal Maxims)

usul ad-din is synonymous with kalam. By *usul al-hadith* is meant the treatment of the terminology and methods of the science of tradition. The *Usul al-Fiqh*, frequently called simply (science of the) *usul*, are the doctrine of the principles of Muslim jurisprudence.[16]

Usul al-Fiqh, which literally means the roots or principles of *Fiqh*, is described as the 'knowledge or science of those rules which directly or proximately lead to the science of *Fiqh*; and hence it discusses the nature of the sources or authorities (i.e. of law) and what appertains thereto, and of the nature of what is established by those sources or authorities, namely, law and what appertains thereto.' As included in the last part of the definition, the discussion relates to the law-giver (*hakim*), the law (*hukm*) and the objectives of law (*mahkum bihi)*, i.e., acts, rights, and obligations, and the subjects of the law, i.e., those to whom the law applies (*mahkum 'alayhi*) or persons.[17]

Fiqh (literally, understanding or knowledge) according to Abu Hanifa, is the knowledge of what is for (*lahu*) a man's self, and what is against (`*alayhi*) a man's self.

---

[16] Gibb, H.A.R., and Kramers, J.H., *Shorter Encyclopaedia of Islam*, Karachi: South Asian Publishers, 1981, p. 611, col. ii

[17] Rahim, Sir Abdur, *The Principles of Muhammadan Jurisprudence*, London: Luzac & Co., 1911, p. 48.

It is the science of rights and obligations of man.

The author of al-Taudih[18] gives the definition of *Fiqh* as the knowledge of the laws (*ahkam*) of the *shari`at*, which are intended to be acted upon, and have been divulged to us by revelation or determined by concurrent decisions of the learned, such knowledge being derived from the sources of the laws with the power of making correct deductions therefrom.

Hukm (law) is that which is established by a communication (*khitab*) from God with reference to men's acts, expressive either of demand or indifference on His part, or being merely declaratory.

Shari`at means the injunctions of the Holy Qur'an and Sunnah covering all human actions. *Fiqh* deals with legal aspects.

Dr. Muhammad Hashim Kamali says:

"To deduce of the rules of *Fiqh* from the indications that are provided in the sources is the expressed purpose of *usul al-Fiqh*. *Fiqh* as such is the end product of *usul al-Fiqh* and yet the two are separate disciplines. *Fiqh* is concerned with the knowledge of the detailed rules of Islamic law in its various branches and *usul al-Fiqh* are concerned with the methods that are applied in the deduction of such rules from their sources. *Fiqh* is the law itself whereas *usul al-Fiqh* is the methodology of the law. The relationship between the two disciplines resembles that of the rules of grammar to the

---

[18] It is a summary of *Usul al-Bazdawi, al-Mahsul,* and the *Mukhtasar al-Muntaha* of the Maliki jurist, Abu `Umar `Uthman bin al-Hajib (*d.* 646AH) written by Sadr al-Shari`ah, `Abdullah bin Mas`ud al-Bukhari (*d.* 747AH).

language or the rules of the logic to philosophy. *Usul al-Fiqh* provide standard criteria for the correct deduction of the rules of *Fiqh* from the sources of *shari`ah*. An adequate knowledge of *Fiqh* necessitates close familiarity with its sources. The knowledge of the rules of *Fiqh* must be acquired directly from the detailed evidence in the sources, a requirement which employs that the *faqih* must be in contact with the sources of *Fiqh*. Consequently, a person who learns the *Fiqh* in isolation from its sources is not a *faqih*. The *faqih* must know not only the rule that misappropriating the property of others is forbidden but also the detailed evidence for it in the source, i.e., the Qur'anic verse (2:188) which provides *"Devour not each others' property in defiance of the law."* This is the detailed evidence as opposed to saying merely that theft is forbidden in the Qur'an."[19]

The discipline of *Usul al-Fiqh* is also different from the discipline of *Usul al-Qanun* although the two disciplines have much in common with one another. For example, in the case of the law of property, both the disciplines are concerned with the sources of the law of property and not with the detailed rules governing transfer of ownership or regulating the contract of sale. These are the subjects which fall within the scope of the law of property, not the methodology of law. *Usul al-Fiqh* is mainly concerned with the Holy Qur'an, the Sunnah of the Holy Prophet (peace and blessings of Allah (swt) be upon him), the *Ijma`* and the *Qiyas*. A rule of law or a *hukm shar`i* may not be originated outside the general scope of its authoritative sources on grounds, for example, of rationality (`aql) alone. For `aql is not an independent source of law in Islam. *Usul al-Fiqh* is founded in Divine

---

[19] Kamali, Dr. Muhammad Hashim, *Principles of Islamic Jurisprudence*, Selangor Darul Ehsan: Pelanduk Publications, 1989, p.2.

ordinances and the acknowledgement of God's authority over the conduct of man.

Usul al-Qanun, on the other hand, consists mainly of rationalist doctrines, and reason alone may constitute the source of many a secular law. Some of these are historical sources, such as Roman Law or British Common Law, whose principles are upheld or overruled in the light of the prevailing socio-economic conditions of society. The sources of *Shari`ah*, on the other hand, are permanent in character and may not be overruled on grounds of either rationality or the requirement of social conditions. There is admittedly a measure of flexibility in *usul al-Fiqh* which allows for necessary adjustment in the law to accommodate social change. But in principle the *shari`ah* and its sources can neither be abrogated nor could the be subjected to limitations of time and circumstance

He further says:

"The maxims of *Fiqh* referred to a body of abstract rules which are derived from the detailed study of the *Fiqh* itself. They consist of theoretical guidelines in the different areas of *Fiqh* such as evidence, transactions, matrimonial law, etc. As such they are an integral part of *Fiqh* and they are totally separate from *usul al-Fiqh*. Over 200 legal maxims have been collected and compiled in works known as *al-ashbah wa al-naza'ir*; one hundred of these have been adopted in the introductory section (i.e., the first 100 articles) of the Ottoman Majallah (swt). The name '*qawa`id al-Fiqhiyyah*' may resemble the expression, *usul al-Fiqh*, but the former is not a part of the latter and the two are totally different from one another."[20]

Qawa 'idu'l-Fiqh (legal maxims) and Dawabit (principles dealing with a particular subject)

A *Qa'idah* (maxim) is a fundamental juristic principle that applies to the particulars of all subjects or most of the subjects, as the legal maxim *al-'umuru bi maqasidiha* (the affairs are to be judged by the objectives behind them) is applicable almost all the chapters of jurisprudence. Its application is seen in the chapter of ablution (*wudu*), prayer (*salat*), fast (*saum*), poor due (*zakat*), pilgrimage (*hajj*), marriage (*nikah*), divorce (*talaq*), sale (*bay'*) and purchase (*ishtira'*), etc.

A *dabitah* is a principle which relates to a particular chapter or a particular subject falling under that chapter. For instance, the chapter dealing with *'ibadat* or the subject only dealing with zakat.

The example of a *dabitah* is that among the Hanafi jurists the well-known *dabitah* is that once a supererogatory act of worship is started, it becomes necessary to complete it (*lazama'l-nafl bi'l-shuru'i*). This *dabitah* applies to all the subjects like prayer, fasting, pilgrimage, sacrifice of animals. But all these are the subjects of *'ibadat*. Another example is that the status of a citizen of a non-Muslim state who enters into a Muslim territory with temporary permission is the same which is of a non-Muslim permanent citizen of a Muslim state (*al-musta'manu bi manzilati'l-zimmi fi darina*).

---

[20] *ibid.*, p. 7.

It is also a *dabitah* that this *dabitah* is applicable under the discussion of international law (whether public or private) its application is not needed in many other chapters of *Fiqh*.

Legal Position of Maxims

A maxim is not a law. It is also not a source of law. It is not even a basis for any permanent argument as such. This does not mean that to argue on the basis of a legal maxim or to apply it to a new problem is invalid. To use it as an argument and to apply it in the solution of a new problem is valid with the difference that an argument based on it could be called an argument allegorically. The reason is that it is not the argument based on any source of law (*daleel shar'i*). The status of this argument is in fact that of a derivative (*tafri'*). As when a general value is known it becomes easy to know its details or sub-details. Likewise, to know the details or sub-details of legal maxims become easy. According to Dr. Mustafa Ahmad al-Zarqa':

"Hiya dasatiru li'l-tafqih la nusus li'l-qada."
"The legal maxims or the principles of making a person a jurist and to create in him deep discernment of *Fiqh*. These are not the legal texts (nusus) to serve as a basis for judicial decisions."

The Mejelle Commission, who submitted its report to His Majesty, The Sultan of Turkish Empire on 18th *Zilhijjah*, 1285AH / 1st April, 1869AD wrote in it as under:[21]

"On reading it, your Highness will remark that the second part of the prologue consists of rules of the *Fiqh* collected by Ibn Nejim and the lawyers who followed his way of thinking. The judges of the Sher' Court cannot

---

[21] Tyser, C. R. and others, *The Mejelle* (Being an English Translation of *Majallahel-Ahkam-i-Adliyah*), Lahore: All Pakistan Legal Decisions, 1967, p. v.

give judgement by these alone until they find an authority (*naql sarih*).

"But their use is great for the acquisition of the precepts of the *Fiqh* and those, who have studied them possess knowledge of the precepts and the reasons for them, and the other officials can have recourse to them in every case. By these, too, a man can make his affairs conform, as nearly as possible, with the Sher` Law. Consequently, they are put as a prologue and are not written as a book or a chapter with a title."

While discussing the *Qiyas*, *Allamah* Muhammad Iqbal in his famous book Reconstruction of Religious Thought in Islam writes:

The fourth basis of *Fiqh* is *Qiyas*, i.e., the use of analogical reasoning in legislation. In view of different social and agricultural conditions prevailing the countries conquered by Islam, the school of Abu Hanifah seem to have found, on the whole, little or no guidance from the precedents recorded in the literature of traditions. The only alternative open to them was to resort to speculative reason in their interpretations. The application of Aristotelian logic, however, though suggested by the discovery on new conditions in Iraq, was likely to prove exceedingly harmful in the preliminary stages of legal development. The intricate behavior of life cannot be subjected to hard and fast rules logically deducible from certain general notions. Yet, looked at through the spectacles of Aristotle's logic, it appears to be a mechanism pure and simple with no internal principle of movement. Thus, the school of Abu Hanifah tended to ignore the creative freedom and arbitrariness of life, and hoped to build a logically perfect legal system on the lines of pure reason. The legists of Hijaz, however, true to the practical genius of their race, raised strong protests against the scholastic subtleties of the legists of

Iraq, and their tendency to imagine unreal cases which they rightly thought would turn the Law of Islam into a kind of lifeless mechanism. These bitter controversies among the early doctors of Islam let to a critical definition of the limitations, conditions, and correctives of *Qiyas* which, though originally appeared as a mere disguise for the *Mujtahid's* personal opinion, eventually became a source of life and movement in the Law of Islam. The spirit of the acute criticism of Malik and Shafi`i on Abu Hanifah's principle of *Qiyas*, as a source of law, constitutes really an effective Semitic restraint on the Aryan tendency to seize the abstract in preference to the concrete, to enjoy the idea rather than the event. This was really a controversy between the advocates of deductive and inductive methods in legal research. The legists of Iraq originally emphasized the eternal aspect of the 'notion', while those of Hijaz laid stress on its temporal aspect. The latter, however, did not see the full significance of their own position, and their instinctive partiality to the legal tradition of Hijaz narrowed their vision to the 'precedents' that had actually happened in the days of the Prophet and his companions. No doubt they recognized the value of the concrete, but at the same time they eternalized it, rarely resorting to *Qiyas* based on the study of the concrete as such. Their criticism of Abu Hanifah and his school, however, emancipated the concrete as it were, and brought out the necessity of observing the actual movement and variety of life in the interpretation of juristic principles. Thus the school of Abu Hanifah which fully assimilated the results of this controversy is absolutely free in its essential principle and possesses much greater power of creative adaptation than any other school of Muhammadan Law. But, contrary to the spirit of his own school, the modern Hanafi legist has eternalized the interpretations of the founder or his immediate followers much in the same way as the early critics of Abu Hanifah eternalized the decisions given on concrete cases. Properly understood and applied, the essential principle of this school, i.e., *Qiyas*, as Shafi`i rightly says, is only another name for *Ijtihad* which, within the limits of the revealed texts, is absolutely free; and its importance as a principle can be seen from the fact that, according to most of the doctors, as Qadi Shaukani tells us, it was permitted even in the lifetime of the Holy Prophet. The closing of the door of *Ijtihad* is pure fiction suggested partly by the crystallization of legal thought in Islam, and partly by that intellectual laziness which, especially in the period of spiritual decay, turns great thinkers into idols. If some of the later doctors have upheld this fiction, modern Islam is not bound by this voluntary surrender of intellectual independence. Zarkashi writing in the eight century of the Hijrah rightly observes:

'If the upholders of this fiction mean that the previous writers had more facilities, while the later writers had more difficulties, in their way, it is, nonsense; for it does not require much understanding to see that *ijtihad* for later doctors is easier than for the earlier doctors. Indeed the commentaries on the Koran and sunnah have been compiled and multiplied to such an extent that the *Mujtahid* have been compiled and multiplied to such an extent that the *Mujtahid* of today has more material for interpretation than he needs.'

This brief discussion, I hope, will make it clear to you that neither in the foundational principles nor in the structure of our systems, as we find them to-day, is there anything to justify the present attitude. Equipped with penetrative thought and fresh experience the world of Islam should courageously proceed to the work of reconstruction before them. This work of reconstruction, however, has a far more serious aspect than mere adjustment to modern conditions of life. The Great European War bringing in its wake the awakening of Turkey–the element of stability in the world of Islam–as a French writer has recently described her, and the new economic experiment tried in the neighborhood of Muslim Asia, must open our eyes to the inner meaning and destiny of Islam. Humanity needs three things to-day–a spiritual interpretation of the universe, spiritual emancipation of the individual, and basic principles of a universal import directing the evolution of human society on a spiritual basis. Modern Europe has, no doubt, built idealistic systems on these lines, but experience shows that truth revealed through pure reason is incapable of bringing that fire of living conviction which personal revelation alone can bring. This is the reason why pure thought has so little influenced men, while religion has always elevated individuals, and transformed whole societies. The idealism of Europe never became a living factor in her life, and the result is a perverted ego seeking itself through mutually intolerant democracies whose sole function is to exploit the poor in the interest of the rich. Believe me, Europe to day is the greatest hindrance in the way of man's ethical advancement. The Muslim, on the other hand, is in possession of these ultimate ideas on the basis of a revelation , which, speaking from the inmost depths of life, internalizes its own apparent externality. With him the spiritual basis of life is a matter of conviction from which even the least enlightened man among us can easily lay down his life; and in view of the basic idea of Islam that there can be no further revelation binding on man, we ought to be spiritually one of the most emancipated peoples ion earth. Early Muslims emerging out of the spiritual slavery of pre-Islam Asia were not in a position to realize the true significance of this basic idea. Let the Muslim of today appreciate his position, reconstruct his social life in the light of ultimate principles and evolve, out of the hitherto partially revealed purpose of Islam, that spiritual democracy which is the ultimate aim of

Islam."[22]

---

[22] Iqbal, Allamah Muhammad, *The Reconstruction of Religious Thought in Islam*, 2nd edn., Lahore: Institute of Islamic Culture, 1989, pp. 140-2.

Methodology adopted by the Federal *Shari'at* Court and the *Shari'at* Appellate Bench of the Supreme Court in discovering whether a provision of an existing law is against the injunctions of Islam

The methodology which the courts (Federal *Shari'at* Court and the *Shari'at* Appellate Bench of the Supreme Court) apply to discover whether a provision of existing law is or is not against the injunctions of Islam. The steps taken are:[23]

1. To find in the first instance, the relevant verse or verses in the Holy Qur'an regarding the question in issue;

2. In the absence of a direct verse covering the matter to search for a relevant hadith (traditions of the Holy Prophet (peace and blessings of Allah (swt) be upon him) which may apply in the matter;

3. Where a direct verse of the Holy Qur'an or a hadith is not available, try to discover the intent of the Qur'an on the subject from the traditions of the Holy Prophet (peace and blessings of Allah (swt) be upon him) in similar situation;

4. In the absence of the above, ascertain the opinions of and views

---

[23] Shah, Mr. Justice Dr. Nasim Hasan (former Chief Justice of Pakistan), *Islamization of Law in Pakistan*, Islamabad: Shari'ah Academy (Publication No. 1), International Islamic University, 1992, p.7.

adopted by all jurists of renown on that matter and examine their reasoning in order to determine and try to harmonize them to the present day requirements and see whether it is possible to synthesize them with the demands of the modern age; and

5. Attempt to discover and apply, as a last resort, any other option which is consistent and in harmony with the Holy Qur'an and Sunnah.

The last mentioned two modes were adopted even earlier by judges in Pakistan while deciding cases coming up before them. Thus, in the case of Mst. Rashida Begum v. Shahab Din (PLD 1960 Lah. 1142), Mr. Justice Muhammad Shafi` opined:–

"In understanding the Qur'an one can derive valuable assistance from the commentaries written by different learned people of yore, but then is that all? Those commentaries can not be said to be the last word on the subject. Reading and understanding the Qur'an implies the interpretation of it and the interpretation of it in its turn includes the application of it which must be in the light of the existing circumstances and the changing needs of the world.... If the interpretation of the Holy Qur'an by the commentators who lived thirteen or twelve hundred years ago is considered as the last word on the subject, then the whole Islamic society will be shut up on an iron cage and not allowed to develop along with the time. It will then cease to be a universal religion and will remain a religion confined to the time and place when and where it was revealed..."

"With great humility, I venture to submit that it would bot be correct to lay it down as a positive rule of law that the present-day courts in this country should have no power or authority to interpret the Holy Qur'an in a way different from that adopted by the earlier jurists and Imams. The adoption of such a view is likely to endanger the dynamic and universal character of the religion and law of Islam. At the same time it is clear that the views of the earlier Imams and jurists are entitled to the utmost respect, and no court or commentator would differ from them except for very compelling and sound reasons...."

The latest exposition on this subject is contained in the judgement of the *Shari`at* Appellate Bench of the Supreme Court in Pakistan v. Public at Large (PLD 1986 SC 240), and it has been observed:

"We do not feel that while expounding the Injunctions of Islam a possibility of some marginal so-called divergences might be visualized. It is a very difficult and perilous exercise. It can lead to proper and improper consequences. Be that as it may, no such expounding of the Injunctions of Islam will be permissible which does not pay attention to the statement of the text of the Holy Qur'an and Sunnah and to its interpretation together with its khamir and zamir. Within this framework while "expounding" the Injunctions the court will remain under a duty in case of need during a new approach or to meet a new situation to keep in view the following essentials amongst others:

1. Whether instead of attempting a relaxation of an Islamic rule, the relaxation may not be made in the required need for which the relaxation is intended to be made. A very simple exercise preliminary though, will be of great advantage–to ask oneself:

Cannot the society exist or progress without the relaxation and where the answer is negative to ask the further question: Cannot it be done with a temporary and mildest one?

2. It is often said that modernism (even when used in good sense of: achievement, progress and high attainment for the ummah), *Ijtihad* is essential. There can be no cavil with the proposition, but before doing the same within accepted spheres and under well-recognized rules it should also be asked: whether the same objects cannot be achieved without doing it; and, whether purpose would not be served by doing the similar *ijtihad* or making a deviation in the demands of modernism. In other words, cannot the society change towards Islam?

3. Whether a relaxation is approvable on the accepted rules and principels of *ijtihad* and *ijma`*, old or new; zaroorat or zarar; tawil or takhsis, `urf and other recognized methods like *Qiyas*, ihsan, istehsan, masaleh, mursalah, etc.?

4. Whether in case a new principle like the foregoing, is visualized there is support for the same in the Holy Qur'an and the Sunnah?

5. Whether there has been a need similar to the one in issue earlier– if so, whether attempts were made by those who were qualified to do the exercise and with what result; the same would apply to attempts made in all other lands?

6. Whether there are precedents for guidance in the well-known

authentic works–if so, what are the reasons for not following them. It is pertinent to note here that the Pakistani Courts when interpreting and applying laws do follow the precedents if they are by law, binding. And even when not so binding, help is always sought from good precedents. Not only this but also it is well-known, the judgements and opinions of foreign judges and jurists are accepted as legitimate guide or support for resolution of controversies. If that is treated as permissible, (rather indispensable by some at least for the time being) there should be no hesitation in examining the judgements and precedents from our own masters including *Sahaba*, *A'imma* and `*Ulema*, old and new.

7. When examining, views and opinions of the old, special place is to be given to the Khulafa-e-Rashidin and the companions and Tabi`ins in accordance with the Holy Qur'an and Sunnah. It is high time, we reduce the dangers of sectarianism and make masterly combination of both (old and new) with gradual elimination of uncalled for criticism and taboos against the so-called Taqleed and so-called Tajdid, when looking for and following the precedents.

8. It would also be necessary when rendering an answer for a new situation to see whether the interests of Islam and Muslim Ummah are advanced in Islamic way. The collective conscience of the Islamic Ummah, past and present, is also to be kept in view in making answer.

9. Whether after doing the necessary exercise and after going through the above stages and others which might be spelt out later, the question when asked from the spiritual and mental faculties of oneself through Nafs Basira, Nafs Lawwamah and Nafs Mutma'innah and not the Nafs Ammarah the answer comes in the clear affirmative for the intended attempt or step. (See footnote Nos. 5810 and 5819 of Text Translation & Commentary on The Holy Qur'an by `Abdullah Yusuf `Ali (vol. II, III). If not, it must be given up.

10. In unoccupied field, the precedent of Mu`az bin Jabal should be applied with full consciousness of its limitations which can in the present day context, be spelt out from the foregoing points.

Exceptions to The Legal Maxims

As most of the legal maxims are probable or applicable to the most of the particulars of a problem and not to all the particulars, hence, those are not such fundamental principles that can be declared as all encompassing or that there is no scope of any exception to them. There are many causes of such exceptions to a legal maxim. Sometimes, a specific matter comes under altogether a different maxim. Sometimes, there is a special requirement of a legal maxim but the analogy or juristic preference demand the application of some other maxim, in view of which the objectives of *shari'ah* can be achieved by application of some other rule. Still further, sometimes, the application of a legal maxim is put to restriction for the sake of justice, equity, expediency, removal of injury, and inconvenience etc.

Looking into the exceptions to the maxims, it should not be taken for granted that the academic or juristic status of these maxims is doubtful. The fact is that despite these exceptions, the academic significance, juristic status and rank and the role they play in creating legal insight render the legal maxims a distinct status. By knowing these maxims, one has an access to the foundations on which the building of Islamic jurisprudence stands. If a person knows all or most of the legal maxims, he gets a key to solve many legal problems. Those who study the Islamic jurisprudence ignoring these fundamental principles, to them the entire store of *Fiqh* appears to be disintegrated, unsystematic and unorganized collection of values. Thus, they are unable to get acquaintance with the basic trend and philosophy of Islamic *Shari'ah* in the field of legislation.

Imam Abu al-'Abbas Qarafi, a renowned Maliki jurist who has the status of an Imam in the science of furuq has said:

"In the whole treasure of Islamic *Fiqh*, the legal maxims have got a very important place and their advantage cannot be denied academically. The more a person will obtain perception and insight in the legal maxims, the more he will excel in understanding Islamic jurisprudence, the more sound will be his legal opinions. As against this, if a person ignores the legal maxims and remember only the particulars and details of the problems he will have to face great difficulties, inconvenience, and complexities. It is so because the particulars and details are unlimited. But a person who will be fully conversant with the fundamental principles and then attend to the particulars, he may not, in most of the cases, remember the particulars separately. The reason is that the most of the particulars are included in the fundamental principles with which he has already become well-conversant. Another benefit will be that the problems and matters which appear to others as unconnected or disintegrated, will be remembered by such a person easily being contained in a well-nit and systematic scheme.[24]

The theory of jurisprudence (*al-nazariyyah al-Fiqhiyyah*) is different from the juristic principle (*al-Qa`idah al-Fiqhiyyah*). The theory is such big principle whose subject matter is general under which fall many subject matters that are mutually resembling in essential elements (*arkan*), conditions (*shara'it*), and general values (*al-ahkam al-`ammah*) as a theory of contract and a theory of annulment. In other words, the theory is different from the principle in two aspects, viz.:

---

[24] Ghazi, Justice Dr. Mahmud Ahmad, *Qawa`id Kulliyyah aur un ka Aghaz wa Irtiqa'*, Islamabad: Shari`ah Academy, International Islamic University, 1992 (Publication no. 3), pp. 22-24.

1. Legal Maxim per se indicates towards the juristic value and thereafter this value includes all the issues falling under it. For instance, the legal maxim is: Certitude is not faded by suspicion. The juristic value proved by this principle applies to all such problems in which Certitude and suspicion are in conflict with each other. As against this, the juristic theory per se does not carry any legal maxim. For example, theory of ownership, theory of repeal, theory of annulment etc.

2. Legal Maxim does not consist of conditions and essential elements while for a juristic theory the existence of both of them is necessary.

View of Joseph Schacht On Legal Maxims In Traditions

Joseph Schacht says:

"To sum up, legal maxims are rough and ready statements of doctrine in the form of slogans, sometimes rhyming or alliterating. They are not uniform as to provenance and period, and some important ones are rather late. But as a rule they are earlier than traditions, and they gradually take on the form of traditions. They date, generally speaking, from the time of the first primitive systematization of Muhammadan law in the first half of the second century AH, but often represent a secondary stage of doctrine and practice. Some maxims express counter doctrines and unsuccessful opinions, but if sufficiently well attested, they were harmonized with the prevailing doctrine. Also the traditionists used them occasionally, in the form of traditions, for voicing their point of view. Numerous maxims originated in Iraq, and they were sometimes taken over by the Medinese; but we find no traces of the opposite process. This shows the prevalent role of the Iraqians in the early period of Muhammadan jurisprudence. The legal maxims reflect a stage when legal doctrine was not yet automatically put into the form of traditions.

I do not exclude the possibility that some legal maxims may be older than the second century AH or may even go back to the pre-Islamic period, but this cannot be assumed but must be positively proved in each case, as R. Brunschvig has done for the maxim al-wala' li'l-kubr (in Revue Historique de Droit Francais et Etranger, 1950, 23-34)."[25]

---

[25] Schacht, Joseph, *The Origins of Muhammadan Jurisprudence*, Oxford: Clarendon Press,

Kinds Of Legal Maxims

a. Agreed upon principles; and

b. The principles regarding which there is proof of conflict of opinion among the leading jurists of the four schools of thought; or between the scholars of a single school of thought; or there is conflict of opinion in the matter of branches / issues of the problems.

The examples of agreed upon Legal Maxims are:

1. *Al-'umuru bi maqasidiha* (The affairs are to be adjudged according to their objectives);

2. *I'imalu'l-kalami aula min ihmalihi* (It is preferred that effect should be given to a word rather than no effect should be given to it). In other words, as far as possible, for a word to have a meaning it must not be regarded as meaningless, that is to say, without effect;

3. *Al-yaqinu la yazulu bi'l-shakki* (With doubt certitude does not fade).

The examples of the principles regarding which there is conflict of

1975, pp.188-9.

opinions between leading jurists of the four schools of thoughts or between the scholars of a single school of thought or in respect of branches are:

1. *hali'l-`ibratu bi sighi'l-`uqudi au ma`aniha*
   (Whether the words of contracts or their meanings will be relied upon?);

2. *hali'l-`ibratu bi'l-hali awi'l-ma'ali*
   (Whether the present state or the consequence will be relied upon?);

3. *al-nadiru hal yalhaqu bi jinsihi au bi nafsihi*
   (Whether a rare adjoins its species or itself?)

Ibn Rushd in his Bidayah al-*Mujtahid* and Ibn al-Hajib in his *Al-Mukhtasar al-Fiqhiyy* has mentioned such basic principles.

Advantages Of The Legal Maxims

There are many advantages of the juristic principles, such

1. Creation of juristic skill in a person who argues concerning any juristic problem. He becomes able to find out the *shari`ah* value (*hukm*) in respect of many juristic problems.

2. Combining of different branches and particulars of juristic problems that are lying scattered in volumes of books and in different chapters.

3. Comprehension of the objectives of the *Shari`ah* and their implications.

In other words, particulars stated thereunder clearly indicate towards the objectives of the *Shari`ah*, e.g., the juristic principle *al-dararu yazalu* which means a harm shall be removed. This principle shows that the removal of an injury or harm or loss or inconvenience is a great objective amongst the objectives of the *Shari`ah*, i.e., the Islamic Law.

Sources Of Legal Maxims

The sources of legal maxims are:

1. The Holy Qur'an

For example, the legal maxim al-mushaqqatu tajlibu al-taysir (A hardship brings ease) is derived from the Qur'anic verse

إِنَّ مَعَ الْعُسْرِ يُسْرًا

"Lo! With hardship goeth ease"   [TMQ As-Sharh : 6]

Dr. M. Rashid Ahmad Khan says:

"Most of the legal maxims used in different legal systems of the world tally with each other as they are based on rules of natural justice. Islam being the religion of nature also recognizes all those legal maxims which are based on the rules of natural justice. There are a number of Qur'anic verses where the laws laid down in different legal maxims have been described. The following are some of the instances of this nature:

1. No one should be condemned unheard.

The Holy Qur'an says:

وَلَقَدْ خَلَقْنَاكُمْ ثُمَّ صَوَّرْنَاكُمْ ثُمَّ قُلْنَا لِلْمَلَائِكَةِ اسْجُدُوا لِآدَمَ فَسَجَدُوا إِلَّا إِبْلِيسَ لَمْ يَكُن

مِّنَ السَّاجِدِينَ قَالَ مَا مَنَعَكَ أَلَّا تَسْجُدَ إِذْ أَمَرْتُكَ ۖ قَالَ أَنَا خَيْرٌ مِّنْهُ خَلَقْتَنِي مِن نَّارٍ

وَخَلَقْتَهُ مِن طِينٍ قَالَ فَاهْبِطْ مِنْهَا فَمَا يَكُونُ لَكَ أَن تَتَكَبَّرَ فِيهَا فَاخْرُجْ إِنَّكَ مِنَ الصَّاغِرِينَ

"It is We Who created you And gave you shape; Then We bade the angels Bow down to Adam, and they Bowed down; not so Iblis, He refused to be of those Who bow down. (Allah (swt)) said: "What prevented Thee from bowing down When I commanded thee?" He said: "I am better Than he: Thou didst create Me from fire and him from clay." (Allah (swt)) said: "Get thee down From this: it is not For thee to be arrogant, Here get out, for thou Art of the meanest (of creatures)." [TMQ Al-Araaf : 11-13]

In the above verses the following stages are manifest:

a. Opportunity of defense was given.

b. Show cause notice to *Iblis* to explain his conduct.

c. His reply was obtained, considered and found unsatisfactory.

d. Punishment announced.

2. Retrospective punishment is unlawful. it means that no punitive act can be enforced with effect from the retrospective days. It is found in the verse of the Holy Qur'an:

وَمَا كُنَّا مُعَذِّبِينَ حَتَّىٰ نَبْعَثَ رَسُولًا

"...nor would We Visit with Our Wrath Until We had sent an apostle (to give warning)." [TMQ Al-Israa : 15]

No act of omission and commission can be made Permissible from a retrospective date.

3. Necessities are estimated according to their quantity. We cannot inflict injury in self-defense more than which is required. The Holy Qur'an says:

إِنَّمَا حَرَّمَ عَلَيْكُمُ الْمَيْتَةَ وَالدَّمَ وَلَحْمَ الْخِنزِيرِ وَمَا أُهِلَّ بِهِ لِغَيْرِ اللَّهِ ۖ فَمَنِ اضْطُرَّ غَيْرَ

بَاغٍ وَلَا عَادٍ فَلَا إِثْمَ عَلَيْهِ ۚ إِنَّ اللَّهَ غَفُورٌ رَّحِيمٌ.

"He hath only forbidden you Dead meat, and blood, And the flesh of swine, And that on which Any other name hath been invoked Besides that of Allah (swt), But if one is forced by necessity, Without wilful disobedience, Not transgressing due limits,- Then is he guiltless. For Allah (swt) is Oft-Forgiving, Most Merciful. [TMQ Al-Baqarah : 73]

4. A thing permitted on account of an excuse (`uzr) becomes unlawful on the cessation of the excuse. For example, a minor is not liable until he attains the age of majority. In other words, when he is major, the excuse of minority is not available to him. The Holy Qur'an says:

وَابْتَلُوا الْيَتَامَىٰ حَتَّىٰ إِذَا بَلَغُوا النِّكَاحَ فَإِنْ آنَسْتُم مِّنْهُمْ رُشْدًا فَادْفَعُوا إِلَيْهِمْ أَمْوَالَهُمْ ۖ

وَلَا تَأْكُلُوهَا إِسْرَافًا وَبِدَارًا أَن يَكْبَرُوا ۚ وَمَن كَانَ غَنِيًّا فَلْيَسْتَعْفِفْ ۖ وَمَن كَانَ فَقِيرًا

فَلْيَأْكُلْ بِالْمَعْرُوفِ ۚ فَإِذَا دَفَعْتُمْ إِلَيْهِمْ أَمْوَالَهُمْ فَأَشْهِدُوا عَلَيْهِمْ ۚ وَكَفَىٰ بِاللَّهِ حَسِيبًا

"Make trial of orphans Until they reach the age Of marriage; if then ye find Sound judgment in them. Release their property to them."

[TMQ An-Nisa : 6] [26]

2. The Sunnah

For example, the legal maxim *al-'umuru bi maqasidiha* (the affairs are to be adjudged by their objectives) is derived from the following hadith *mutawatar* of the Messenger of Allah (swt) (peace and blessings of Allah (swt) be upon him)

إِنَّمَا الأَعْمَالُ بِالنِّيَّةِ

"Certainly, actions are to be adjudged by the motives behind them."

[Sahih, al-Bukhari, on the authority of *Hadhrat* 'Umar bin al-Khattab Allah (swt)'s pleasure be on him), *Bab Kayfa Kana Bada'ul Wahyi.*]

Similarly, the legal maxim *al-yaqinu la yazulu bi'l-shakki* (the certitude does not fade by doubt) has been derived from the following hadith:

"Iza wajada ahadu kum fi batnihi shay'an fa ashkala akhraja minhu shay'un au la fala yakhrujunna mina'l-masjidi hatta yasma'a sautan au yajida rihan."

"When any one of you finds anything in his belly and doubts as to whether anything has come out or not? He shall not come out of the mosque unless he hears any sound or finds any smell."

---

[26] Dr. M. Rashid Ahmad Khan, Islamic Jurisprudence, Lahore, 1993 pp. 57-59. The translation of the Holy Qur'an has been taken from 'Abdullah Yusuf 'Ali as the same has been taken at all other places in this book

[Al-Nazariyat al-`Ammah li'l-ma`amalat fi'l-*shari`ah* al-Islamiyyah, p.4]

3. Circumstance (*qarinah*)

The legal maxim *yuftaqaru fi'l-baqa'i ma la yuftaqaru fi'l-ibtida'i* (That which is not in need of anything in the beginning becomes in need of it for survival).

Books On Legal Maxims

The leading jurists of Hanafi school of thought compiled the following books on the Legal Maxims:

1. *Al-'usul*, al-Karkhi, Abu'l-Hasan `Ubaydullah bin Husain (260-340AH)

2. *Ta'sis al-Nazar,* al-Dabbusi, `Ubaydullah bin `Umar (d. 430AH).

3. *Al-Ashbah wa'l-Naza'ir*, Ibn Nujaym, Zaynu'l-`Abidin, Ibrahim al-Misri (d. 970AH).

4. *Majami` al-Haqa'iq*, al-Khadimi, Muhammad bin Sa`id (d. 1176AH).

5. *MujAllah al-Ahkam al-`Adaliyyah,* prepared by the Council of Jurists constituted by Amir al-Mu'minin Sultan `Abd al-`Aziz al-`Uthmani (d. 1293AH). This was the law enforced in Turkish Ottoman Empire and remained in force till 1342AH / 1928AD.

6. *Al-Fawa'id al-Bahiyyah fi'l-Qawa`id al-Fiqhiyyah*, Afandi, Sayyid Mahmud, the Mufti of Damascus (d. 1305AH).

The leading jurists of Maliki school of thought compiled the following books on Legal Maxims:

1. *'Usul al-Futya*, al-Khashni, Muhammad bin Harith bin Asad (d. 362 AH).

2. *Anwar al-Buruq fi Anwa' al-Furuq*, al-Qarafi, Shahabuddin Ahmad bin Idris (d. 684AH).

3. *Tahzib al-Furuq wa'l-Qawa`id al-Sanniyyah fi al-Asrar al-Fiqhiyyah*, Maliki, Muhammad `Ali bin Husain, the Mufti of Makkah al-Mukarramah (d. 1367AH).

4. *Al-Manhaj al-Muntakhab `ala Qawa`id al-Mazhab*, al-Zaqqaq, Abu'l-Hasan `Ali bin Qasim (d. 912AH).

5. Idah *al-Masalik ila Qawa`id Imam Malik*, al-Wansharisi, Ahmad bin Yahya (d. 914AH).

6. *Al-Majaz al-Wadih*, Haudi (al-Wala'i), Muhammad Yahya bin Muhammad al-Mukhtar bin Talib. (This is in the form of a long poem.)

The leading jurists of Shafi`i school of thought compiled the following books on Legal Maxims:

1. *Qawa`id al-Ahkam* fi Masalih al-Anam, `Izzuddin bin `Abd al-`Aziz `Abd al-Salam (d. 660 AH).

2. Al-Ashbah wa'l-Naza'ir, Sadruddin, Muhammad bin `Umar

bin Wakil Abi `Abdullah (d. 716AH).

3. Al-Ashbah wa'l-Naza'ir, Subki, Tajuddin `Abd al-Wahhab bin `Ali bin `Abd al-Kafi (d. 771AH).

4. Al-Manthur fi al-*Qawa`id*, Zarkashi, Badruddin Muhammad bin Bahadur Shafi`i (d. 794AH).

5. Al-Ashbah wa'l-Naza'ir fi *Qawa`id* wa Furu` al-Shafi`iyyah, Suyuti, Imam Jalaluddin `Abd al-Rahman (d. 911AH).

The leading jurists of Hanbali school of thought compiled the following books on Legal Maxims:

1. *Al-Qawa`id al-Nuraniyyah*, Ibn Taymiyyah, Ahmad (d. 728AH).

2. *Al-Qawa`id wa'l-Fawa'id al-'usuliyyah wa ma Yata`allaqu biha min al-Ahkam al-Far`iyyah*, Ibn al-Lahham al-`Abali al-Hanbali, Abu'l-Hasan `Aliyyuddin, `Ali bin `Abbas (d. 752AH).

3. *Taqrir al-Qawa`id wa Tahrir al-Fawa'id*, Hanbali, `Abd al-Rahman bin Rajab (d. 795AH).

4. Mughni *Zu'l-Afham `an al-Kutub al-Kathirah fi'l-Ahkam*, Maqdasi, Yusuf bin `Abd al-Hadi Hanbali (d. 909AH).

Maxims Under Latin And Anglo-Saxon Law

The English word maxim is derived from the Latin word maxima, which means a general principle. Its synonyms are axiom, aphorism, apothegem, adage, proverb, saying, a leading truth.

It is a piece of wisdom or advice expressed in a sentence. It is a fundamental truth. It is a rule by which conduct may be guided. Conduct is what a man does. Character is what one is, i.e., his moral and personal qualities (his nature). When a man's conduct is noble, he also bears a good moral character.

In Latin, the word maxime has been defined as

Maxime, so called *quia maxima est ejus dignitas et certissima auctoritas, atque quod maxime omnibus probetur* (Co. Litt. 11a) – *Maxime*, so called because its dignity is chiefest and its authority the most certain and because universally approved by all.

General Legal Maxims, though they have their own use and are of considerable importance in the administration of justice, cannot supersede statutory provisions. [223 IC 93].

Much valuable works have been published by the English authors collecting many legal maxims which are also of great use in the matter of legal problems.

In *Latin For Lawyers*, 3rd ed. 1960, published by Sweet & Maxwell,

London, a worldwide renowned law publisher, the merit of the maxim has been very beautifully summed up at p. 105 in the following words:

Law, like moral philosophy or politics has its maxims which sum up in a pregnant sentence some leading principle or axiom of law; so called, says Coke, "quia maxima est ejus dignitas et certissima auctoritas atque quod maxime omnibus probetur." The merit of the maxim is twofold. It is a useful generalization of law wherein every student who would become his gown may note, as Wingate says, how the same key opens many locks, or, to put it in another way, how all the cases are reducible to a few theses. The other merit of the maxim lies in its epigrammatic form. Like the proverb, it embodies "the wisdom of many and the wit of one".

These qualities of the maxim–its sententiousness and its epigrammatic point–have made it at all times a favourite form of legal currency, tendered and accepted generally–or, to take another metaphor, a portable armoury of legal weapons. Nowhere more than in its maxims does the robust good sense of the common law of England display itself. At any rate one of the maxims warn the critic that no one ought to be wiser than the laws–"*Neminem oportet legibus esse sapientiorem.*"

The maxims of English law, like the rules of the common law, derive their source and sanction from an immemorial antiquity, from frequent judicial recognition, and from the imprimatur of the sages of our law. One writer, indeed–Wingate–has gone so far as to describe them as "prime emanations of the Eternal Wisdom". Their usefulness may be said to increase, rather than to diminish, as the law grows more complex and involved, for they bring back the mind to first principles."

Mr. Salmond says:

"Legal maxims are the proverbs of the law They have the same merits and defects as other proverbs, being brief and pithy statements of partial truths. They express general principles without the necessary qualifications and exceptions and they are therefore much too absolute to be taken as trustworthy guides to the law. Yet they are not without their uses.

The language of legal maxims is almost invariably Latin, for they are commonly derived from the Civil law, either literally or by adaptation, and most of those which are not to be found in the Roman sources are the invention of medieval jurists." [Jurisprudence, p. 498]

In the introduction to the *Legal Maxims*, Mr. Broom says:

"In the ruder ages, without doubt, the great majority of questions respecting the rights remedies and liabilities of private individuals were determined by an immediate reference to such maxims, many of which obtained in the Roman Law, and are so manifestly founded on reason, public convenience and necessity, as to find a place in the code of every civilization."

Life Sketch Of The Author

His name is ʿUbaidullah bin al-Hasan bin Dallal bin Dalham. His title is Abu al-Hasan and he is well known as al-Karkhi. He was born at Karkh Jaddan in the year 260AH during the caliphate of al-Muʿtamid ʿalAllah (swt) al-ʿAbbasi (256-279AH) and died at Baghdad on the night of 15th of Shaʿban, 340AH / 952AD during the caliphate of al-Mutiʿ lillah al-ʿAbbasi (334-363AH).

The word Karkh is an Arabicised word of Persian word Charkh, which means a water-mill. After Baghdad was built, the area in which those water-mills were installed was known as al-Karkh. One such water-mill was owned by Jaddan and the whole block was popular with the name Karkh Jaddan. It was this block in which parents of ʿUbaydullah lived and he was born there. Imam Abu Yusuf Yaʿqub bin Ibrahim al-Karkhi (Allah (swt)'s mercy be on him), the pupil of Imam Abu Hanifah (Allah (swt)'s mercy be on him) had after coming from Kufa had settled in this block. Imam Abu Yusuf (Allah (swt)'s mercy be on him) died in the year 182AH.

He learnt al-*Fiqh* from Ahmad bin al-Husayn Abu Saʿid al-Burdaʿi (a great jurist of Baghdad and one of the leading jurists of the earlier times who died in the year 317AH), who learnt *Fiqh* from Ismaʿil bin Hammad, who learnt it from his own father and who learnt it from his grand father al-Imam al-Aʿzam Abu Hanifah al-Nuʿman (Allah (swt)'s mercy be on all of them).

From him al-*Fiqh* was learnt by Abu Bakr al-Razi al-Jassas and Abu `Abdullah al-Damighani and Abu `Ali al-Shashi and Abu al-Qasim `Ali bin Muhammad al-Tannukhi and Ahmad al-Tabari, Abu `Abdullah al-Jurjani, Abu Zakariyya al-Darir al-Basari, Abu `Abdullah al-Mu`tazali and others (Allah (swt)'s mercy be on all of them).

His name has been repeatedly referred to in al-Hidayah and on him terminated the chain of leading jurists after Abu Hazim and Abu Sa`id al-Burda`i. His own companions spread all over the world.

He was among the highly excellent category of those who are known as *al-Mujtahidin fi'l-masa'il*. He wrote many books and among them the most popular are the following:

1. *Al-Mukhtasar fi'l-Fiqh*
2. *Sharh al-Jami` al-Kabir li'l*-Imam Muhammad bin Hasan al-Shaybani (d. 189AH)
3. *Sharh al-Jami` al-Saghir li'l*-Imam Muhammad bin Hasan al-Shaybani (d. 189AH)
4. *Al-Usul*

He was a contemporary of the great leading muhaddithin viz., Imam Ibn Majah, Imam Abu Da'ud, Imam Abu 'Isa Tirmizi, Imam Abu Hatim Razi, Imam Darimi, Imam Abu Zar'ah Damishqi, Imam Bazzaaz, Imam Nisa'i, Imam Abu Ya`la Al-Musili and Imam Abu 'Uwanah (Allah (swt)'s mercy be on all of them). Among the well known jurist his contemporaries were Imam Abu Ja`far Tahawi and Imam Abu Dawud Zahiri (Allah (swt)'s mercy be on them). In the presence of these highly esteemed and well known leading men of knowledge the people of his time had recognized Imam Karkhi as a great jurist and there was consensus of all that he was the greatest Hanafi jurist of his time.

He was a person who was content, pious, devoted, often observing fasts and establishing prayers. He was repeatedly offered the office of Chief Justice of the state but he declined the same and earned his livelihood with his own hands. He was an institution in himself and disseminated the sciences of *tafsir*, hadith, and *Fiqh* to the students without charging a single penny from them. People had great respect and profound regard for him. At the close of his life span, he had an attack of paralysis and his companions wrote a letter to *Sayf al-Daulah* bin Ahmad of which he came to know and wept and prayed to God Almighty:

"O God! Do not make for me a sustenance except that which Thou hast Thyself provided me".

The prayer was accepted and he died prior to the reaching of an amount of ten thousand dirhams from *Sayf al-Daulah*.

According to al-Sam`ani, he was known as al-Karkhi due to his domicile in Karkh, a town in the suburbs of Iraq.

Life Sketch Of The Commentator

His name was 'Umar bin Muhammad bin Ahmad bin Isma'il bin Muhammad bin Luqman al-Hanafi. His titles were Mufti al-Thaqalayn Najmuddin Abu Hafs al-Nasafi. He was born in the year 460AH/1067AD in Nasaf, which was a city between Samarqand and the river Jihun (*Balad al-Nahr*) and died on 12 Jamadi al-'Ula, 537AH / 1142AD in Samarqand.

He was a leading jurist, highly learned, well-versed in the sciences of '*usul*, *kalam*, *tafsir*, hadith, *Fiqh* and grammar. He was one of the well-known leading jurists who had enormous memory and was very popular both among the masses and those who had command in knowledge. He learnt *Fiqh* from Sadr al-Islam Abu al-Yusr Muhammad al-Buzdawi, who learnt it from Abu Ya'qub Yusuf al-Sayyari, who learnt it from Abu Ishaq al-*Hakim* al-Nauqadi, who learnt it from al-Hindawani, who learnt it from Abu Bakr al-A'mash, Abu Bakr al-Askaf, and Abu'l-Qasim al-Saffar. And al-A'mash from Abu Bakr al-Askaf from Muhammad Ibn Salmah from Abu Sulayman al-Juzjani from Muhammad (Allah (swt)'s mercy be on all of them). And Al-Saffar from Nasir bin Yahya from Muhammad bin Sama'ah from Abu Yusuf from al-Imam al-A'zam Abu Hanifah (Allah (swt)'s mercy be on all of them).

He wrote nearly one hundred books on the subjects of *tafsir*, *Fiqh*, 'aqa'id and among his prominent writings are:

1. *Al-Taysir fi'l-Tafsir*
2. *Al-'Aqa'id al-Nasafiyyah* (which is prevalent with commentary of

al-Taftazani)

3. *Al-Manzumah* (which is the first book composed on the subject of al-*Fiqh*)

4. *Kitab al-Mawaqit*

5. *Qayd al-Awabid*

6. *Talabah al-Tulabah fi Lughat al-Fuqaha* (which is a commentary of the difficult words of the books of Hanafi doctors)

7. *Al-Ash`ar bi'l-Mukhtar min'l-Ash`ar* (in 20 volumes)

8. *Kitab al-Mushari`*

9. *Qand fi ``Ulama' Samarqand*

10. *Al-Akmal al-Atwal*

11. *Tarikh* Bukhara

It is stated that he wrote nearly one hundred books. He had many teachers from whom he got knowledge. A group of scholars have attained the knowledge of *Fiqh* from him and the author of Hidayah recited to him some of his writings.

Imam Abu Hafs 'Umar al-Nasafi has mentioned under each legal principle enunciated by Imam al-Karkhi, instances, precedents, and proofs, so that each principle becomes clear and easy to understand and to apply it for solving the problems. In this manner, it has become a commentary of the original book.

It is stated that he used to teach both the jins and the human beings. And it was for this reason that he was called Mufti al-Thaqalayn. It is also stated that he intended to visit Jarullah al-Zamakhshari, who was in Makkah al-Mukarramah and when he took his step, he reached his door and knocked it.

Zamakhshari asked, "*man haza?*" He replied, "'Umar". Zamakhshari said, "*insarif*". Najmuddin said, "*ya Sayyidi 'Umaru la yansarifu*". Zamakhshari said, "*iza nakara sarafa*"

Undoubtedly, Imam al-Nasafi was a great jurist, highly learned of Hanafi school of thought and well-versed in literature.

Arabic Text, Transliteration of Arabic into English, English translation and al-Nasafi's commentary containing the examples and translator's notes

In the name of Allah (swt), the Beneficent, the Merciful.

All praise is to Allah (swt) and peace and blessings of Allah (swt) be upon our leader *Hadhrat* Muhammad and on his family and companions.

Maxim 1

الْأَصْلُ: أَنَّ مَاثَبَتَ بِالْيَقِينِ لَا يَزُوْلُ بِالشَّكِّ

Al-aslu anna ma thabata bi al-yaqini la yazulu bi al-shakki

The basic rule is that which is established by certainty is not faded by doubt.

Commentary

According to Imam Abu Hafs 'Umar al-Nasafi, the problems covered by this maxim include the problem that where a person is in doubt in the matter of the state of his being pure and clean and he is certain that he has performed ablution (*wudu*) then he will be taken as in a state of purity and cleanliness as he is not sure about the breaking of the ablution (*wudu*).

On the other hand, where a person is sure that he is without ablution (*wudu*) and by conjectures he considers himself to be in ablution (*wudu*), then he will be taken in a state of being without ablution (*wudu*).

Translator's Note

The reason being that a judgment is not to be based on conjectures and surmises.

Maxim 2

الْأَصْلُ: أَنَّ الظَّاهِرَ يَدْفَعُ الِاسْتِحْقَاقَ وَلَا يُوْجِبُ الِاسْتِحْقَاقَ

Al-aslu anna al-zahira yadfa'u al-istihqaq wa la yujibu al-istihqaq
The basic rule is that the apparent (state) can be a defense against any claim of right but it does not establish a right.

Commentary

Where a person is in possession of a house and a man brings a suit against him. On the basis of the apparent state that the possession is of the defendant, the claim of the plaintiff will not be accepted till he proves it before the judge by means of two creditworthy witnesses. In case the house is sold to a neighbor and the plaintiff wants to get the house sold through a suit for pre-emption on the plea of neighborhood of the said house and the defendant denies such plea that he is owner of it, the plaintiff shall have no right of pre-emption unless he establishes by legal evidence that the adjacent house is in his ownership.

Maxim 3

الْأَصْلُ: أَنَّ مَنْ سَاعَدَهُ الظَّاهِرُ فَالْقَوْلُ قَوْلُهُ والْبَيِّنَةُ عَلَى مَنْ يَدَّعِيْ خِلَافَ الظَّاهِرِ

Al-aslu anna man sa`adah al-zahir fa al-qaulu qaulu hu wa al-bayyinatu
`ala man yad`i khalaf al-zahiri

The basic rule is that the statement of apparently assisted shall have preference, the burden of proof lies on him who claims against the apparent.

Commentary

Where a person claims his debt being payable by the debtor and the guarantor and the defendant denies it, his statement will be relied upon and the burden of proof shall be on the person who is claiming against the apparent state.

Maxim 4

الْأَصْلُ: أَنَّهُ يُعْتَبَرُ فِي الدَّعَاوِي مَقْصُودُ الْخَصْمَيْنِ فِي الْمُنَازَعَةِ دُوْنَ الظَّاهِرِ

Al-aslu annahu ya`tabiru fi al-da`awi maqsud al-khasmayn fi al-
manaza`ah duna al-zahir

The basic rule is that in claims the objective of the parties in the litigation shall be relied upon and not the apparent.

Commentary

Where a depositor demands return of the deposit and the creditor states that he has already returned the amount while the depositor states that he has not returned it, the statement of the receiver of the deposit shall be relied upon as he is claiming the apparent by stating that he has returned it. It is so because the object is the guarantee while he is denying the guarantee. Therefore, his statement shall be relied upon.

Maxim 5

الْأَصْلُ: أَنَّ الظَّاهِرَيْنِ إِذَا كَانَ أَحَدُهُمَا أَظْهَرَ مِنَ الْآخَرِ فَالْأَظْهَرُ أَوْلَى لِفَضْلِ ظُهُورِهِ

Al-aslu anna al-zahirayn iza kana ahaduhuma azharu min al-akhiri fa al-azharu 'ula bi fadli zahuri hi

The basic rule is that where there are two apparent states and one of them is more apparent than the other, then the more apparent shall have precedence due to its additional manifestation.

Commentary

Where a person makes an admission in favour of an unborn child of a debt, then according to Imam Muhammad (Allah (swt)'s mercy be on him) such an admission in favour of the said child by the said person is valid even if there is possibility (*ihtimal*) of doubt.

According to Imam Abu Yusuf (Allah (swt)'s mercy be on him) it is not valid. The reason is that his clear admission about the debt would make a contract binding upon him which was not otherwise binding on him. As a contract with an unborn child is not valid. And if he clearly stated that he has destroyed his property and compensation is binding on him, his admission shall be valid. Where he makes a brief statement, there occurs a doubt in the matter of binding. Therefore, it will not become binding.

But Imam Muhammad's (Allah (swt)'s mercy be on him) view is based on the apparent state of a sane Muslim, i.e., when he makes a statement, he intends to make a valid statement and he is bound by it. Therefore, the admission regarding the destruction of the property is valid.

On the other hand, Imam Abu Yusuf (Allah (swt)'s mercy be on him) has stated that by such an admission, nothing becomes binding on him. It is so because he is on the apparent state that is more apparent than that. The reason is that the apparent state of the sane Muslim is that he does not destroy the property of another person as it is a sin.

Maxim 6

الْأَصْلُ: أَنَّ أُمُورَ الْمُسْلِمِينَ مَحْمُولَةٌ عَلَى السَّدَادِ وَالصَّلَاحِ حَتَّى يَظْهَرَ غَيْرُهُ

Al-aslu anna 'umur al-muslimina mahmulatun `ala al-sidadi wa al-salahi
hatta yazharu ghayru hu

The basic rule is that the affairs of the Muslims shall bear solidarity and well-being unless appears otherwise.

Commentary

Where a person sells a dirham and a dinar for two dirhams and two dinars, the sale will be considered as valid by applying the principle of exchange of one kind with another kind and keeping in view the bona fide and correctness of action of a Muslim. But if there is legal proof that there had been sale of a dirham for two dirhams and sale of a dinar for two dinars (of the same kind) it would render the sale invalid. It is so because it is clearly against the apparent.

Maxim 7

الْأَصْلُ: أَنَّ لِلْحَالَةِ مِنَ الدَّلَالَةِ كَمَا لِلْمَقَالَةِ

Al-aslu anna li al-halati min al-dalalati kama li al-maqalati

The basic rule is that an oral statement will be taken as the circumstances require.

Commentary

Where a person deposits goods with another person and the said person returns it to a member of his family in whose possession the said goods are destroyed, he shall not be liable to pay compensation even if he had not clearly granted permission to return it to any one besides him. It is so because when he deposits such goods with him with the knowledge that he will not be able to protect them while in his possession during day or night it would be taken as an indication of grant of permission from him that he will protect the goods as he would have protected his own goods. And it is commonsense that he will protect his own goods sometimes by his own possession and sometimes by giving it under the possession of his family member. And the later becomes like a clear permission in that behalf from his side.

The immediate or emergent problems are based on this principle.

Maxim 8

الْأَصْلُ: أَنَّهُ قَدْ يَثْبُتُ مِنْ جِهَةِ الْفِعْلِ مَا لَا يَثْبُتُ مِنْ جِهَةِ الْقَوْلِ كَمَا فِي الصَّبِيِّ

Al-aslu anna hu qad yathbutu min jihati al-fi`l ma la yathbutu min jihati al-qauli ka ma fi al-sabiyyi

The basic rule is that a thing is established by an act that was not established by a word as is in the case of a minor.

Commentary

Where a person appoints an other person as his agent or attorney by an agreement, if he removes his agent in his absence by oral statement, the agent shall not stand removed till he gets knowledge of his removal. In such a case if an agent acts according to his power of attorney before getting knowledge of withdrawal of such power, his exercise of power shall be enforced and if the principal exercises his own control in such session himself without knowledge that the agent has been removed by fiction of law regarding enforcement of exercise of his power in the matter in respect of which he was appointed an agent.

The statement of the author, "like a minor" means that the minor shall be liable to pay compensation for his act even if he is not liable to pay compensation for the loss caused on account of his word that is on account of an oral agreement or guarantee or admission / acknowledgement.

Maxim 9

الْأَصْلُ: أَنَّ السُّؤَالَ وَالْخِطَابَ يَمْضِيْ عَلَى مَا عَمَّ وَغَلَبَ لَا عَلَى مَا شَذَّ وَنَدَرَ

Al-aslu anna al-su'ala wa al-khitaba yamdi `ala ma `amma wa ghalaba la `ala ma shazza wa nadara.

The basic rule is that a question and an address are to mean that which is common and probable and they do not mean that which is rare and casual.

Commentary

Where a person swears that he will not eat an egg. His statement will be taken to mean that he will not eat an egg of a bird. It will not be taken to mean that he will not eat an egg of fish.

Maxim 10

الْأَصْلُ: أَنَّ جَوَابَ السُّؤَالِ يَجْرِيْ عَلَى حَسْبِ مَا تَعَارَفَ كُلُّ قَوْمٍ فِيْ مَكَانِهِمْ.

Al-aslu anna jawab al-su'ali yajri `ala hasbi ma ta`arafa kullu qaumin fi makani him

The basic rule is that the answer of a question shall be according as to the custom of a people of their country.

Commentary

Where a person takes an oath that he will not take any food. Thereafter he drinks milk he will become guilty of breaking his oath even by it while he is in the Arab countries but not in non Arab countries. The reason is that the food of each people is that which they consider as food by their custom, habit or usage.

Maxim 11

الْأَصْلُ: أَنَّ الْمَرْءَ يُعَامَلُ فِي حَقِّ نَفْسِهِ كَمَا أَقَرَّ بِهِ وَلَا يُصَدَّقُ عَلَى إِبْطَالِ حَقِّ الْغَيْرِ
وَلَا بِإِلْزَامِ الْغَيْرِ حَقًّا

Al-aslu anna'l-mar'a yu`amilu fi haqqi nafsi hi ka ma aqqarra bi hi wa la
yusaddiqu `ala ibtali haqqi al-ghayri wa la bi ilzami al-ghayri haqqan.

The basic rule is that a man is bound to act according to his own acknowledgement. He will not be taken as true in the matter of cancellation of the right of another person nor by his statement another person can be bounded regarding any right.

Commentary

Where the parentage (*nasab*) of a female is not known and she makes an acknowledgement that she has freed a person and the said person testifies her statement she will be considered his female slave but the marriage shall not become void with the husband nor the husband will be liable to pay compensation to the person in whose favour acknowledgement is made when he had paid her the dower once.

Where a depositee who is appointed to return the deposit says that he has returned it to a certain person and the said certain person states that he has not returned it to him, the statement of the depositee shall be relied upon in the matter of discharge of liability from him of paying compensation. But his statement regarding acceptance of compensation against a person in possession shall not be relied upon.

Maxim 12

الْأَصْلُ: أَنَّ الْقَوْلَ قَوْلُ الْأَمِيْنِ مَعَ الْيَمِيْنِ مِنْ غَيْرِ بَيِّنَةٍ

Al-aslu anna al-qaula qaulu al-amini ma` al-yamini min ghayri bayyinatin

The basic rule is that the statement of a trustee along with oath shall be reliable in the absence of legal evidence / proof.

Commentary

All claims of a depositee regarding the return of the deposit to the depositor / owner or its destruction while in his custody and likewise all trustees like the lendees (*al-musta`ir*), sleeping partners (*al-mudarib*) and agents (*al-wakil*).

Maxim 13

الْأَصْلُ: أَنَّ مَنِ الْتَزَمَ شَيْئًا وَلَهُ شَرْطٌ لِنُفُوْذِهِ فَإِنَّ الَّذِيْ هُوَ شَرْطٌ لِنُفُوْذِ الْآخَرِ يَكُوْنُ فِي الْحُكْمِ سَابِقًا وَالثَّانِيْ لَاحِقًا وَالسَّابِقُ يَلْزَمُ لِلصِّحَّةِ وَالْجَوَازِ

Al-aslu anna man iltazama shay'an wa la hu shartun li nufuzi hi fa inna allazi huwa shartun li nufuzi al-'akhiri yakunu fi al-hukmi sabiqan wa al-thani lahiqan wa al-sabiqu yalzimu li al-sihhati wa al-jawazi

The basic rule is that where a man makes a thing binding and there is a condition for its being effective, then the condition of last effectiveness will be precedent and the second will be subsequent and the fulfillment of the condition precedent shall be necessary for validity and permissibility.

Commentary

Where offering of prayer becomes compulsory on a person, the performance of ablution becomes compulsory for him as it is a condition precedent for prayer.

Maxim 14

الْأَصْلُ: أَنَّ الْمُتَعَاقِدَيْنِ إِذَا صَرَّحَا بِجِهَةِ الصِّحَّةِ صَحَّ الْعَقْدُ وَإِذَا صَرَّحَا بِجِهَةِ الْفَسَادِ
فَسَدَ، وَإِذَا أَبْهَمَا صُرِفَ إِلَى الصِّحَّةِ

Al-aslu anna al-muta`aqidayna iza saraha bijihati al-sihhati sahha al-`aqda wa iza saraha bi jihati al-fasadi fasada wa iza abhama sarafa ila al-sihhati

The basic rule is that where the two contracting parties explicitly stated the validity, the contract shall be valid; where both the parties to the contract explicitly stated the irregularity, the contract shall be irregular / invalid; and where both the contracting parties made ambiguous statements, the contract shall be taken as a valid contract.

Commentary

Where a person sells a silver instrument of the weight of ten and a cloth of the price of ten in lieu of twenty dirhams on the condition that ten out of those shall be deferred in payment till one month and if he explicitly states that the ten deferred relate to the price of cloth and the ten in cash relate to the price of the silver instrument it is valid contract. But if he explicitly stated that it is the price of the silver instruments it is an invalid / irregular contract. If they both made ambiguous statements and declare the ten cash dirhams for the instrument and the deferred for the cloth their statements will be taken as valid contract.

Maxim 15

الْأَصْلُ: أَنَّهُ يُفَرَّقُ بَيْنَ الْفَسَاد إِذَا دَخَلَ فِي أَصْلِ الْعَقْدِ وَبَيْنَهُ إِذَا دَخَلَ فِي عَلَقَةٍ مِنْ عَلَائِقِهِ

Al-aslu anna hu yafruqu bayna al-fasadi iza dakhala fi asli al-`aqdi wa bayna hu iza dakhala fi `alaqatin min `ala'iqi hi

The basic rule is that the irregularity that enters in the root of the contract and the irregularity that enters in any thing related to the contract shall be differentiated.

Commentary

Where a person sells a slave for one thousand dirhams and a weight (ratl) of wine the sale shall be invalid but if he excludes the wine even then the validity shall not be there as the invalidity (al-fasad) lies in the root of the contract. And where a person sells a slaves for a consideration of one thousand dirhams on payment deferred till the harvest of the crop, the contract of sale shall be invalid for not knowing the actual time and if the said stipulation is excluded before the approach of the time of harvest the contract will revert to validity as it is a stipulation attached to the contract.

Maxim 16

الْأَصْلُ: أَنَّ الضَّمَانَاتِ فِي الذِّمَّةِ لَا تَجِبُ إِلَّا بِأَحَدِ أَمْرَيْنِ إِمَّا بِأَخْذٍ أَوْ بِشَرْطٍ فَإِذَا عَدَمَا لَمْ تَجِبْ

Al-aslu anna al-damanat fi al-zimmati la tajibu illa bi ahadi al-'amarayni amma bi akhzin au bi shartin fa iza `adama lam tajib

The basic rule is that the liability for payment of compensation does not become obligatory save in the presence of any of the following two circumstances, viz., Holding of a thing; or Existing of a stipulation.

Where none of these circumstances exists, the liability shall not be obligatory.

Commentary

The holding of a thing refers to extortion (*al-ghasb*), possession by mortgage (*qabd al-rahn*), finding an unclaimed thing without evidence (*iltiqat min ghayr ish-had*).

The stipulation refers to the acceptance of the contract like purchase (*al-shira'*) and lending (*al-istijar*) and guaranty (*al-kafalah*) etc.

Maxim 17

الْأَصْلُ: أَنَّ الِاحْتِيَاطَ فِي حُقُوقِ اللهِ تَعَالَى جَائِزٌ وَفِي حُقُوقِ الْعِبَادِ لَا يَجُوزُ

Al-aslu anna al-ihtiyata fi huquqi Allah (swt)i ta`ala ja'izun wa fi huquqi al-`ibad la yajuzu

The basic rule is that precaution is permissible in the matter of rights of

God while it is not permissible in the matter of rights of men.

Commentary

Where the question revolves around the validity and irregularity in the matter of the offering of the prayer, the rule of precaution is that it should be again offered. It is so because it is better to offer even when there is no such liability than to abandon.

Where the question revolves around the permissibility and non-permissibility in the matter of liability to pay compensation (al-daman), the rule of precaution is not mandatory. The reason is that such a liability does not accrue in the presence of doubt.

Maxim 18

الْأَصْلُ: أَنَّهُ يُفَرَّقُ فِي الْأَخْبَارِ بَيْنَ الْأَصْلْ وَالْفَرْعِ

Al-aslu anna hu yafraqu fi al-akhbari bayna al-asli wa al-far`i
The basic rule is that a distinction will be drawn in the matter of information between the root and the branch.

Commentary

Where a woman is informed of suckling (al-rada`at) between spouses, separation shall not be ordered between them and distinction will be drawn in the matter of branch by declaring it a divorce or a khul`.

Maxim 19

الْأَصْلُ: أَنَّهُ يُفَرَّقُ بَيْنَ الْعِلْمِ إِذَا ثَبَتَ ظَاهِرًا وَبَيْنَهُ إِذَاثَبَتَ يَقِينًا.

Al-aslu anna hu yafruqu bayna al-`ilmi iza thabata zahiran wa bayna hu iza thabata yaqinan

The basic rule is that a distinction will be drawn in the matter of knowledge when it is established apparently and when it is established certainly.

Commentary

Where a thing comes to knowledge certainly to believe and act upon it is obligatory and that which is established apparently to act upon it is obligatory but to believe in it is not obligatory.

To clarify this point, reference can be made to the five daily regular prayers and the *witr*.

Both ears are part of head as is known apparently, but to consider wiping of both of them as compulsory wiping is not permissible.

The Hatim is part of Baytullah Sharif as is known apparently but to face towards it while offering the prayer and to keep the Baytullah Sharif at back side is not permissible as the direction towards Baytullah Sharif is compulsory which is established by certainty.

Where a judge decides a case and thereafter it comes to his knowledge, he has committed an error on the basis of an apparent proof but not on the basis of certainty, his judgment shall not be set aside but where his error becomes apparent on the basis of a certain proof of text (Qur'an and Sunnah) and *ijma`*, his judgment shall be set aside.

Maxim 20

الأصل أنه قد يثبت الشيء تبعا وحكما وإن كان قد يبطل قصدا.

Al-aslu anna hu qad yathbitu al-shay'a taba`an wa hukman wa in kana qad yabtulu qasdan

The basic rule is that a thing is established incidentally and legally even if it is cancelled intentionally.

Commentary

Where a principal cancels the power-of-attorney in the absence of such attorney, it shall remain established for exercise of such power in the matter of the things for which such power was given incidentally and if the principal removes the attorney intentionally, it shall not be valid till the attorney gets the knowledge about it. And if he sold a slave, all necessary aspects shall be included in the thing sold incidentally. Likewise, in the sale of a house, the air of the house and likewise, in the sale of the land, the water sources and if he sells the amenities intentionally and also the air and water, it would not be valid. There are many precedents on this point.

Maxim 21

الْأَصْلُ: أَنَّ الْإِجَازَةَ اللَّاحِقَةَ كَالْوَكَالَةِ السَّابِقَةِ

Al-aslu anna al-ijazata al-lahiqata ka al-wakalati al-sabiqati
The basic rule is that a subsequent permission is like a previous agency.

Commentary

Where a person enters into a contract regarding the property or person of another person such as sale, marriage or any other contract without the command (and consent) of such other persons and when such other person receives information of such contract he grants permission, the contract shall be enforced and the person who made such contract is considered as his agent in the matter of that contract.

This is according to the view of Hanafi doctors of law, as against the view of Imam Shafi`i (Allah (swt)'s mercy be upon him).

Maxim 22

الْأَصْلُ: أَنَّ الْمَوْجُودَ فِي حَالَةِ التَّوَقُّفِ كَالْمَوْجُودِ فِي أَصْلِهِ

Al-aslu anna al-maujuda fi halati al-tawaqquf ka al-maujud fi asli hi
The basic rule is that a thing existing in a state of suspension is like a thing existing in original.

Commentary

Extra receipts by the purchaser after the contract when joined by the permission become like those that were present for the purchaser at the time of contract.

Maxim 23

الْأَصْلُ: أَنَّ الْإِجَازَةَ إِنَّمَا تَعْمَلُ فِي الْمُتَوَقِّفِ لَا فِي الْجَائِزِ

Al-aslu anna al-ijazata innama ta'malu fi al-mutawaqqafi la fi al-ja'izi

The basic rule is that the permission operates in suspended and not in the permissible.

Commentary

Where a person is authorized for the purchase of a slave for a consideration of 500 dirhams and he purchases it for 600 dirhams, he will be taken as having bought it for himself and if the person who has authorized him for such purchase, gets information that he has purchased for 600 and gives permission, the person who has authorized shall have no authority to give such permission. It is so because the purchase stood established for the purchaser at the time of its execution / occurrence. Hence the permission shall neither operate in it nor the purchase will be for the said person.

Maxim 24

الْأَصْلُ: أَنَّ الْإِجَازَةَ تَصِحُّ ثُمَّ تَسْتَنِدُ إِلَى وَقْتِ الْعَقْدِ.

Al-aslu anna al-ijazata tasahhu thumma tastanidu 'ila waqti al-'aqdi

The basic rule is that the permission validates a contract and extends itself to the time of actual entrance into it.

Commentary

The subject matter of contract must be presently worthy of a contract so that the contract may be effected in a state of permission and could be taken to the time of existence of the contract. Where the subject matter is destroyed the contract is not enforceable. The permission should be in respect of the existing subject matter and not the destroyed subject matter.

Thus, where at the time of permission, the granter of permission is in his death bed sickness while the contract was made when he was healthy, the exercise of control of the sick will be considered as invalid.

Maxim 25

الْأَصْلُ أَنَّ الْإِجَازَةَ فِي الْقَائِمِ دُونَ الْهَالِكِ

Al-aslu anna al-ijazata fi al-qa'imi duna al-haliki

The basic rule is that a permission is in an existing thing and not in a destroyed thing (object of contract).

Commentary

Where a thing sold by a suspended contract destroys and thereafter the party having authority to contract grants permission, such a permission shall not be enforced.

Maxim 26

الْأَصْلُ: أَنَّ كُلَّ عَقْدٍ لَهُ مُجِيزٌ حَالَ وُقُوعِهِ تَوَقَّفَ لِلإِجَازَةِ وَإِلَّا فَلَا

Al-aslu anna kulla `aqdin la hu majizun hala wuqu`ihi tawaqqufun li al-ijazati wa illa la

The basic rule is that every contract for which there is a an executor, its occurrence shall remain suspended for obtaining permission of the executor otherwise not.

Commentary

Where a persons sells the property of a minor for a consideration of an amount equal to its price, the contract of sale shall remain suspended on the permission of the guardian of the minor. It is so because it is the guardian who has got the authority to sell the property of his ward.

where he divorces his wife or frees slave or gives in charity his property, the contract shall not be suspended as the guardian has no such authority.

Maxim 27

الْأَصْلُ: أَنَّ تَعْلِيقَ الْأَمْلَاكِ بِالْأَخْطَارِ بَاطِلٌ وَتَعْلِيقُ زَوَالِهَا بِالْأَخْطَارِ جَائِزٌ

Al-aslu anna ta`liqa al-amlaki bi al-akhtari batilun wa ta`liqu zawali ha bi al-akhtari ja'izun

The basic rule is that attachment of a condition of danger in the matter of properties is void and the attachment of a condition of its perishing by dangers is valid.

Commentary

Where a person makes an offer to another person: "If you enter in the house I sold this slave to you for one thousand" and the other person says: "I accept" or utters similar words. If such offer and acceptance is in the matter of license / permission (al-'ijazah) and gift (al-hibah) etc. It shall not be valid nor the ownership shall occur in the presence of such condition / stipulation (*al-shart*).

But if he says to his wife: "If you enter the house you stand divorced." or he says to his slave, "If you enter the house, you are free" it shall be valid and in the presence of the condition the divorce and the freedom shall become effective and the ownership of nikah and bondage shall vitiate.

Maxim 28

الْأَصْلُ: أَنَّ الشَّيْءِ يُعْتَبَرُ مَا لَمْ يَعُدْ عَلَى مَوْضُوْعِهِ بِالنَّقْضِ وَالْإِبْطَالِ

Al-aslu anna al-shay'a ya'tabiru ma lam ya'id 'ala maudu'ihi bi al-naqdi wa al-ibtali

The basic rule is that a thing shall have weight unless it is considered as forged by way of being contradictory and void.

Commentary

Where an inhibited slave lends his services for a known period it is not valid to avoid harm to his master. We have given the verdict regarding its irregularity after the expiry of the period. The whole service will be harmful for the master as the benefit which he had to receive would suspend without compensation. Hence here the removal of the injury / harm / loss is required for its validity. If we give the verdict of its irregularity it would not have removed the injury / harm / loss. Rather the loss stood established. Hence the matter of loss is to be considered.

Maxim 29

Al-aslu anna hu iza mada bi al-ijtihadi la yafsakhu bi ijtihadi mithli hi wa yafsukhu bi al-nassi

The basic rule is that where a matter is decided by personal judgment (al-*ijtihad*), it is not cancelled by a similar personal judgment (al-*ijtihad*) and can be set aside only by a text (being contrary to it).

Commentary

This problem occurs in the matter of inquiries and decision of claims.

Maxim 30

الْأَصْلُ: أَنَّ النَّصَّ يَحْتَاجُ إِلَى التَّعْلِيلِ بِحُكْمٍ غَيْرِهِ لَا بِحُكْمٍ نَفْسِهِ

Al-aslu anna al-nassa yuhtaju ila al-ta`lil bi hukmi ghayri hi la bi hukmi nafsi hi

The basic rule is that the text (*nass*) needs justification (*al-ta`lil*) in the matter of a *shari`ah* value (*hukm*) other than itself and not in the matter of its own *shari`ah* value (*hukm*).

Commentary

The unlawfulness of six things is established by the very text (*'ayn'l-nass*), and not by the meanings (*al-m'ani*) of the hadith of the Holy Prophet (peace and blessings of Allah (swt) be upon him) which says:

al-hintatu bi'l-hintati… (wheat for wheat…)
al-sha`iru bi'l-sha`iri… (barley for barley…)
al-tamaru bi'l-tamari… (dates for dates…)
al-milhu bi'l-milhi… (salt for salt…)
al-zahabu bi'l-zahabi… (gold for gold…)
al-fiddatu bi'l-fiddati… (silver for silver…)
mathalun bi mathalin… (like for like…)
yadan bi yadin…   (hand by hand…)
wa'l-fadlu riba'.   (and excess is interest/usury.)

In all those goods which are transacted by measures (*al-makilat*) and by weight (*al-mauzunat*) the unlawfulness is established by the meanings of the hadith (*bi'l-ma`na*), in which both the species (*jins*) and the quantity (*qadr*) are present.

Likewise, it is established in similar things.

Maxim 31

الْأَصْلُ: أَنَّهُ يُفَرَّقُ بَيْنَ عِلَّةِ الْحُكْمِ وَحِكْمَتِهِ فَإِنَّ عِلَّتَهُ مُوْجِبَةٌ وَحِكْمَتَهُ غَيْرُ مُوْجِبَةٍ

Al-aslu anna hu yafruqu bayna `illati al-hukmi wa hikmati hi fa inna `illata hu mujibatun wa hikmata hu ghayru mujibatin

The basic rule is that the effective cause of a *Shari`ah* value and the wisdom lying in it is differentiated. The effective cause is necessary while its wisdom is not necessary.

Commentary

The effective cause of shortening the prayer is the journey and the wisdom behind such shortening is the hardship. Further a journey is a proof of shortening of the prayer even if there is no hardship attached with it. Non-existence of wisdom does not make non-existence of *Shari`ah* value, while existence of an effective cause makes the existence of the *Shari`ah* value obligatory. The effective cause of absolution (*al-istibra*) is occurrence of propriety to use the sex (*milku'l-watyi*) of those whom the right hand of person possesses (*milk yamin*) and wisdom behind it is the protection of parentage (*siyanatu'l-nasab*) and avoidance of mixture of two waters. Thereafter, when a person purchases a virgin or a maid slave from a female or a child, then certain absolution becomes mandatory, whereby the womb is cleared. And non-existence of wisdom does not makes the obligation non-existent where there is found new ownership.

Maxim 32

الْأَصْلُ: أَنَّ السَّائِلَ إِذَا سَأَلَ سُؤَالًا يَنْبَغِيْ لِلْمَسْئُوْلِ أَنْ لَا يُجِيْبَ عَلَى الْإِطْلَاقِ وَالْإِرْسَالِ

لَكِنْ يَنْظُرُ فِيْهِ وَيَتَفَكَّرُ أَنَّهُ يَنْقَسِمُ إِلَى قِسْمٍ وَاحِدٍ أَوْ إِلَى قِسْمَيْنِ أَوْ أَقْسَامٍ ثُمَّ يُقَابِلُ فِيْ

كُلِّ قِسْمٍ حَرْفًا فَحَرْفًا ثُمَّ يُعَدِّلُ جَوَابَهُ عَلَى مَا يَخْرُجُ إِلَيْهِ السُّؤَالُ. وَهَذَا الْأَصْلُ تَكْثُرُ مَنْفَعَتُهُ

لِأَنَّهُ إِذَا أَطْلَقَ الْكَلَامَ فَرُبَّمَا كَانَ سَرِيْعَ الِانْتِقَاضِ لِأَنَّ اللَّفْظَ قَلَّمَا يَجْرِيْ عَلَى عُمُوْمِهِ

*Al-aslu anna al-sa'ila iza sa'ala su'alan yanbaghi li al-mas'uli an la yajibu
`ala al-itlaqi wa al-irsali lakin yanzuru fi hi wa yatafakkaru anna hu
yanqasimu ila qismin wahidin au ila qismayni au aqsamin thumma yuqabilu
fi kulli qismin harfan fa harfan thumma yu`addilu jawabu hu `ala ma
yakhruju `ilay hi al-su'alu wa haza al-aslu takthuru manfa`ata hu li anna hu
iza atlaqa al-kalamu fa rubama kana sari`u al-intiqadi li anna al-lafza fa
lamma yajri `ala `amumi hi*

The basic rule is that when a questioner asks a question, it is befitting for
the questioned that he should not answer absolutely and loosely but should
look into it and consider it if it can be divided into a single part or two parts
or many parts. Thereafter, he should compare each part word by word. Then
he should justify his answer that comes out relevant to the question.

This basic rule has multiple advantages. It is so because when the speech
is absolute, often it comes across accelerated contradiction.

The reason is that a word rarely follows its general sense.

Commentary

This happens in all sorts of acts of worship and ownership and crimes etc.
For example, where a person turns his face for *salam* at the end of two *rak`ats*

of Zuhr prayer, whether his prayer will be invalid or it is stated that he ate something during the state of fasting while he says that he has done so inadvertently or intentionally or when it is stated that a slave sold a thing and he states that he was permitted to do so or inhibited and when it is said that a man killed a man, what will be his liability when he says that he committed that act intentionally or unintentionally or mistakenly or resembling intentionally and by which weapon and when it is stated that a man committed *zina*, what is his liability while he states that he was married (*muhsin*) or unmarried (*ghayr muhsin*) or such other problems. There are many precedents on this point.

Maxim 33

الْأَصْلُ: أَنَّ الْحَادِثَةَ إِذَا وَقَعَتْ وَلَمْ يَجِدِ الْمُؤَوِّلُ فِيْهَا جَوَابًا وَنَظِيْرًا فِيْ كُتُبِ أَصْحَابِنَا فَإِنَّهُ

يَنْبَغِيْ لَهُ أَنْ يَسْتَنْبِطَ جَوَابَهَا مِنْ غَيْرِهَا إِمَّا مِنَ الْكِتَابِ أَوْ مِنَ السُّنَّةِ أَوْ غَيْرَ ذَلِكَ مِمَّا

هُوَ أَقْوَى فَالْأَقْوَى فَإِنَّهُ لَا يَعْدُوْ حُكْمَ هَذِهِ الْأُصُوْلِ

Anna al-hadithata iza waqa`at wa lam yajid al-mu'awwul fi ha jawaban wa naziran fi kutubi ashabi na fa inna hu yanbaghi lahu an yastanbitu jawabu ha min ghayri ha imma min al-kitab au min al-sunnati au ghayra zailik min ma huwa al-aqwa fa al-aqwa fa inna hu la ya`idu wa hukmu hazihi al-usul

Where an event occurs and the interpreter does not find in respect of it any answer or precedent in the books of our doctors of law, he should deduce its answer from other sources. It may be the Kitabullah or sunnah of Rasul Allah (saw) or other sources besides them. The strongest source shall remain the strongest and that will not be out of the rule laid down in this basic principle.

Commentary

Imam Nasafi said that the fixed deduced problems by this rule and the deduction of answers for the new events are included in this principle.

Maxim 34

الْأَصْلُ: أَنَّ اللَّفْظَ إِذَا تَعَدَّى مَعْنَيَيْنِ أَحَدُهُمَا أَجْلَى مِنَ الْآخَرِ وَالْآخَرُ أَخْفَى فَإِنَّ الْأَجْلَى أَمْلَكُ مِنَ الْأَخْفَى

Al-aslu anna al-lafza iza ta`adda ma`niyyayn ahadu huma ajla min al-akhiri wa al-akhiru akhfa fa inna al-ajla amlaku min al-akhfa

The basic rule is that where a word is transitive to two meanings, one of them is more clear than the other and the other is much hidden, then the apparent meaning shall be adopted.

Commentary

Allah (swt) Almighty says:

وَلَٰكِن يُؤَاخِذُكُم بِمَا عَقَّدتُّمُ الْأَيْمَانَ ۖ فَكَفَّارَتُهُ إِطْعَامُ عَشَرَةِ مَسَاكِينَ

...But he will ask you about those of your oaths that you have contracted and the expiation for breaking such oath is to feed ten needy persons...

[TMQ Al-Maidah : 89]

Our doctors of law have taken this contract to mean that which is apparent / more clear. And it is regarding the future. Imam Shafi'i (Allah (swt)'s mercy be on him) has taken it to a contract that is made by resolution of heart and it occurs in the past also while the former is more clear, therefore, it has precedence.

Maxim 35

الْأَصْلُ: أَنَّهُ يَجُوزُ أَنْ يَكُونَ أَوَّلُ الْآيَةِ عَلَى الْعُمُومِ وَآخِرُهَا عَلَى الْخُصُوصِ

Al-aslu anna hu yajuzu an yakuna awwalu al-ayati 'ala al-'umumi wa akhiru ha 'ala al-khususi ka 'aksi hi

The basic rule is that it is permissible that the earlier portion of a verse may be general and the later portion of a verse may be particular like its opposite.

Commentary

Allah (swt) Almighty says:

وَمَن قَتَلَ مُؤْمِنًا خَطَأً فَتَحْرِيرُ رَقَبَةٍ مُّؤْمِنَةٍ وَدِيَةٌ مُّسَلَّمَةٌ إِلَى أَهْلِهِ

...And whosoever murders a believer by mistake, on him is the liability to free a neck of a believer and the payment of blood-wit (diyat) according to the known custom to the entitled...   [TMQ An-Nisa : 92]

At another place in the Holy Qur'an, Allah (swt) Almighty says about a person who embraces Islam in enemy country and does not migrate to the Islamic state:

$$فَإِن كَانَ مِن قَوْمٍ عَدُوٍّ لَّكُمْ وَهُوَ مُؤْمِنٌ فَتَحْرِيرُ رَقَبَةٍ مُّؤْمِنَةٍ$$

...And if he is of the people who are your enemy while he is a believer, then (in case of his murder) the liability is to set free a neck of a believer...

[TMQ An-Nisa : 92]

Here payment of known amount of *diyat* to the entitled (*diyatin musallamatin ila ahlihi*) has not been mentioned.

Allah (swt) Almighty says:

$$فَلَا جُنَاحَ عَلَيْهِمَا أَن يُصْلِحَا بَيْنَهُمَا صُلْحًا ۚ وَالصُّلْحُ خَيْرٌ$$

...There is no harm for both of them if they enter into a compromise and a compromise is better...

[TMQ An-Nisa : 128]

The earlier portion of this verse is in respect of the spouses while the later portion is general and for all the people.

Maxim 36

$$الْأَصْلُ: أَنَّ التَّوْفِيقَيْنِ إِذَا تَلَاقَيَا وَتَعَارَضَا وَفِي أَحَدِهِمَا تَرْكُ اللَّفْظَيْنِ عَلَى الْحَقِيقَةِ فَهُوَ أَوْلَى$$

Al-aslu anna al-taufiqayn iza talaqiya wa ta`arada wa fi ahadi hima tarku* *al-lafzayn `ala al-haqiqati fa huwa 'ula

The basic rule is that where two conformities corroborate and contradict and in one of them there is abandonment of too words on fact, that shall have precedence.

Commentary

One hadith says that the Messenger of Allah (swt) (peace and blessings of Allah (swt) be upon him) said that the menstruating woman shall perform ablution (*wudu*) for every prayer.

The other hadith says that the Messenger of Allah (swt) (peace and blessings of Allah (swt) be upon him) said that the menstruating women shall perform ablution (wudu) for the time of every prayer.

Our doctors of law have acted upon both the above said ahadith and said that the period of her cleanliness shall extend in the time. It is so because in the first hadith there is mention of time and the second hadith carries the meaning that by the prayer the intention is of its time as the Messenger of Allah (swt) (peace and blessings of Allah (swt) be upon him) said that wherever I found the prayer, I performed *tayammum*, i.e., I found the time of prayer.

The statement of Imam Shafi`i (Allah (swt)'s mercy be on him) that she is bound by the prayer is acting upon clearly on the second hadith as the word of time is found in the hadith.

Maxim 37

الْأَصْلُ:أَنَّ الْبَيَانَ يُعْتَبَرُ بِالِابْتِدَاءِ إِنْ صَحَّ الِابْتِدَاءُ وَإِلَّا فَلَا

Al-aslu anna al-bayana ya`tabiru bi al-ibtida'i an sahha al-ibtida'a wa illa fa la

The basic rule is that the validity of a statement is to be seen in the beginning. If it is not so, it is not valid.

Commentary

Where a man has two wives and after consummation of marriage, he states to both of them, "You both are divorced." Thereafter, he says to both of them while they both are observing their `iddat that one of you two is divorced thrice. His statement in respect of both of them shall remain valid as in the beginning he had so stated. Thus, if they both completed their `iddat, there shall be three divorces for each one of them is not valid and the conformity will survive. It is so because if he had begun with it, it was not valid. And if one of them completes the `iddat first, the second shall have the three pronouncements of *talaq* on her.

Bibliography

1. Al-Qur'an al-Majid

– English Translation and Commentary by `Abdullah Yusuf `Ali.

2. Al-Hadith al-Sharif

– `*Umda al-Qari*, Allama Badruddin `Aini.
– *Al-Qaul al-Badi`a*, Allama Sakhawi.
– *Ash`atu'l-Lam`at,*Shaykh `Abd   al-Haqq Muhaddith Dehlawi.
– *Jila al-Afham*, Allama Ibn Qayyim.
– *Mirqat*, Allama Mulla Ali Qari.
– *Mishkat al-Masabih*,   AllamaWaliyuddin Muhammad al-Khatib.
– *Mu'atta*, Imam Malik.
– *Musnad*, Ahmad bin Hanbal, al-Imam.
– *Musnad*, Imam A`zam, Abu Hanifah Nu`man bin Thabit.
– *Riyad al-Salihin*, Abu Zakariyya Yahya bin Sharf al-Nawawi, al-Imam.
– *Sahih*, al-Bukhari, Al-Imam Allama Muhammad Isma`il.
– *Sahih*, Muslim, Imam Abu'l-Husain Muslim bin Hajjaj al-Qushairi.
– *Sunan*, Abu Da'ud Sulayman bin Ash`ath al-Sajistani.
– *Sunan*, al-Nisa'i, Abu Abd al-Rahman Ahmad bin Shu`aib al-Nisa'i.
– *Sunan*, al-Tirmizi, Imam Abu `Isa Muhammad bin `Isa *Tirmizi*.
– Sunan, Ibn Majah, Abu Abdullah Muhammad bin Yazid bin Majah al-Qizwini.

3. Jurisprudence

- *Al-Ashbah wa'l-Naza'ir*, Allama Tajuddin `Abd al-Wahhab al-Subki.
- *Al-Ashbah wa'l-Naza'ir*, Zayn al-`Abidin bin Ibrahim Ibn
- Nujaym.
- *Al-Jauharah al-Nayyirah*, Shaykh al-Islam Abu Bakr bin
- `Ali bin Muhammad al-Haddad al-Yamani.
- *Al-Mabsut*, al-Imam Shams al-Din al-Sarakhsi.
- *Al-Qawa`id al-Fiqhiyyah*, `Abd al-Wahhab Abu Sulayman.
- *Al-Qawa`id*, Abu `Abdullah Muhammad bin Muhammad bin Ahmad al-Muqri.
- *Al-Talwih*, Allama Sa`duddin Taftazani.
- *Al-Wajiz fi 'Usul al-Fiqh*, Dr. Abdul Karim Zaydan, Lahore: Faran Academy, n.d.
- *Badai` al-Sanai`*, al-Imam `Ala'uddin Abu Bakr bin Mas`ud al-Kasani.
- *Fath al-Qadir*, Allama Ibn Hammam Muhammad bin `Abd al-Wahid.
- *Al-Fiqh al-Islami wa 'Adillatahu*, Dr. Wahbah al-Zuhayly, Damascus, Dar al-Fikr, 1996 edn.
- *Fiqh al-Islam*, Hasan Ahmad al-Khatib.
- *Fiqh Hanafi kay Asasi Qawa`id,* Muhamad Anwar Maghalwi.
- *Hidayah*, Allama Burhanuddin `Ali bin Abi Bakr al-Marghinani.
- *Hujjatullahi'l-Balighah*, Shah Waliullah Muhaddith Dehlavi.
- Islamic Jurisprudence, Dr. M.Rashid Ahmad Khan, Lahore: Mansoor Book House, 1993.
- *Islami Fiqh*, Maulana Mujibullah Nadwi.

- *Kanz al-Daqa'iq*, Abu al-Barkat 'Abdullah bin Ahmad bin Mahmud al-Nafasi.
- *Maraqi` al-Falah*, Allama Hasan bin`Ammar bin`Ali al-Sharanbali.
- Philosophy of Shah Waliullah, Dr. Abdul Wahid J. Halepota.
- The Principles of Muhammadan Jurisprudence, Sir Abd al-Rahim, London: Luzac & Co., 1911.
- *Mu`jam Lughat al-Fuqaha*, Dr Muhammad Rawwas Qal`aji and Dr Hamid Sadiq Qunalbi.
- *Nur al-`Idah*, Allama Hasan bin 'Ali al-Sharanbali.
- *Nur al-Anwar*, Mullah Jiwan.
- *Qawa`id al-Fiqh* (comprising five booklets (i) *Usul* al-Imam al-Karkhi, (ii) *Usul* al-Masa'il al-Khalafiyyah alongwith examples as given by Abu Zayd al-Dabbusi in Tasis al-Nazar, (iii) Al-*Qawa`id* al-*Fiqhiyyah*, (iv) Al-Ta`rifat al-*Fiqhiyyah* and (v) Adab al-Mufti, collected and edited by Mufti Sayyid Muhammad `Amim al-Ihsan al-Mujaddidi al-Barkati.)
- *Radd al-Mukhtar*, Allama Muhammad Amin al-Shahir bi Ibn
- `Abidin.
- *Sharh al-Majallah*, Salim Rustam Bar al-Bannani.
- *Sharh Waqayah*, Shaykh `Ubaidullah bin Mas`ud.
- *'Usul*, al-Karkhi, Urdu translation (edn. 1402AH) by `Abd al-Rahim Ashraf Baloch.
- *'Usul al-Fiqh*, Imam Muhammad Abu Zuhrah, Cairo: Dar al-Fikr al-Arabi, 1958.
- *'Usul al-Fiqh*, Shaykh Muhammad al-Khudari Bak, Bayrut, Dar Ahya' al-Turath al-Arabi, 6th edn., 1969.
- *'Usul* al-Shashi, Allama Nizam al-Din al-Shashi.

4. General References

- *Al-Fiqh al-Islami fi Thaubihi al-Jadid*, Allama Mustafa Ahmad al-Zarqa', Damascus, 1963.
- *Al-Munjid al-Abjadi*.
- *Al-Qamus al-`Asri*, Elias A. Elias.
- *Al-Qawa`id, Al-Muqri*, Abu`Abdullah Muhammad bin Muhammad bin Ahmad, Makkah al-Mukarramah.
- Concise Oxford Dictionary, 5th edn, Oxford: Oxford
- University Press, 1996.
- Development of Muslim Theology, Jurisprudence and Constitutional Theory, Macdonald, Duncan B., Lahore:
- Premier Book House, n.d.
- Dictionary of Islam, Hughes, Thomas Patrick, Lahore: Kazi Publications, 1998.
- First Steps in Muslim Jurisprudence, Russull, A.D., and
- Suhrawardy, Abdullah al-Mamun, London: Luzac & Co., 1963.
- *Ghamz `Uyun al-Basa'ir fi Sharh al-Ashbah wa'l-Naza'ir*, Al-Hamawi, Luknow: Nolkashor Press.
- Glosssary of Qur'an and Hadith, M.A. Qazi, Lahore: Kazi Publications, 1998.
- *"Ijtihad aur Mujtahid"*, Mughal, Dr. Munir Ahmad., in Minhaj, vol. I, No. 1, Lahore: Diyal Singh Trust Research Cell, 1983.
- Islamic Jurisprudence, Faruki, Kemal A., Karachi: Pakistan Publishing House, 1962.
- Islamic Jurisprudence: Shafi`i's Risala, Khadduri, Majid.,
- Baltimore: The Johns Hopkins Press, 1961.

- Islamic Jurisprudence, Hanif, Prof. Dr. C. M., Lahore: Syed Mobin Mahmud & Co., 1996.
- Islamic Jurisprudence, Qureshi, M.H., Karachi: Karachi Law publisher, 1978.
- Islamization of Law in Pakistan, Mr. Justice Dr. Nasim Hasan Shah, Islamabad: *Shariah* Academy, 1992.
- Latin for Lawyers, Sweet & Maxwell, 3rd ed., London 1960. Law Terms and Phrases, Sardar Muhammad Iqbal Mokal. Law Terms and Phrases, Muhammad Ilyas.
- Legal Maxims, Brooms.
- Legal Maxims with Observations and Cases, George Frederick Wharton, London 1903.
- *Mu`jam al-Mufahras li Alfaz al-Hadith*.
- *Mu`jam al-Mufahras li alfaz al-Qur'an al-Karim*, Muhammad Fuwad Abd al-Baqi.
- *Mukhtasar Qawa`id al-`Ula'i*, Ibn Khatib al-Dahshanah.
- Pakistan Law Journal. Various issues, Lahore: Punjab Bar Council.
- Pakistan Legal Decisions. Various issues. Lahore: PLD
- Publishers.
- Principles of Islamic Jurisprudence, Muhammad Hashim Kamali, Selangor Dar al-Ehsan: Pelanduk Publications,
- 1989.
- *Qawa`id Kulliyyah* aur un ka Aghaz wa Irtiqa', Mr. Justice Dr. Mahmud Ahmad Ghazi, Islamabad: *Shariah* Academy.
- Reconstruction of Religious Thought in Islam, Allama Muhammad Iqbal.
- Scope of Legal Maxims, Syed Imtiaz ul Haq Naushahi, Lahore: Lahore

Law Times Publishers, 1971.

- *Sharh al-Majallah*, Ibn Rustam Baz.
- Shorter Encyclopaedia of Islam, H.A.R. Gibb and J. H. Kramers, Karachi: South Asian Publishers, 1981.
- The Origins of Muhammadan Jurisprudence, Joseph Shacht, Oxford: Clarendon Press, 1975.